**HOME OFFICE**

# Working with the Third Sector

LONDON: The Stationery Office
£11.25

Ordered by the
House of Commons
to be printed on 27 June 2005

REPORT BY THE COMPTROLLER AND AUDITOR GENERAL | HC 75 Session 2005-2006 | 29 June 2005

This report has been prepared under
Section 6 of the National Audit Act 1983
for presentation to the House of Commons
in accordance with Section 9 of the Act.

*John Bourn*
**Comptroller and Auditor General**
**National Audit Office**

**22 June 2005**

The National Audit Office
study team consisted of:

Grace Williams, Damian Cleghorn,
Tim Pryce and Barbara Carvalho, under the
direction of Joe Cavanagh. The National
Council for Voluntary Organisations
(NCVO) was our research partner. Its
research team consisted of Ann Blackmore,
Karl Wilding, Mubeen Bhutta, Tilly Forster
and Silvie Dresselhaus.

This report can be found on the National
Audit Office web site at www.nao.org.uk

**For further information about the**
**National Audit Office please contact:**

National Audit Office
Press Office
157-197 Buckingham Palace Road
Victoria
London
SW1W 9SP

Tel: 020 7798 7400

Email: enquiries@nao.gsi.gov.uk

# CONTENTS

Photographs courtesy of Red Cross (by David Webb); The Prince's Trust; Volunteering England; The Children's Society; the Home Office; Centrepoint (by Claudia Janke); Community Network for Manchester.
Cover photograph posed by models for The Children's Society

# SUMMARY

1    Public service delivery has often been seen as a choice between direct state provision and the use of the private sector. In many instances, though, the "third sector" (often referred to as the voluntary and community sector) provides an alternative. This report examines how government departments and other funders can best work with the third sector to achieve value for money in public services.

---

**The third sector**

The "third sector" describes the range of institutions which occupy the space between the State and the private sector. These include small local community and voluntary groups, registered charities both large and small, foundations, trusts and the growing number of social enterprises and co-operatives. Third sector organisations share common characteristics in the social, environmental or cultural objectives they pursue; their independence from government; and in the reinvestment of surpluses for those same objectives.[1]

---

2    In recent years the government has recognised that third sector organisations (TSOs[2]) have an important role to play in the drive to improve public service delivery. In some cases TSOs may be best placed to deliver a service, especially where a service needs to connect with clients who are difficult to reach or distrustful of state agencies. TSOs can also have great expertise in their specialist areas, and help develop and pilot innovative solutions to difficult issues. In the right circumstances, TSOs can help deliver a more effective service and provide the taxpayer with better value for money.

3    TSOs already carry out a wide variety of public services funded or part-funded by the taxpayer, such as hospice care for terminally ill patients, childcare services in disadvantaged areas, and advice and guidance for young people. **Figure 1 overleaf** gives some examples of the various ways in which TSOs provide public services.

4    Although the sector is a prominent provider in some areas of public services, it nonetheless accounts for only around 0.5 per cent of central government expenditure.[3] The government has a declared commitment to increasing the role of the third sector in public services. However, both TSOs and government have noted that their relationship is not as effective as it might be. In 1998, a Compact on relations between the government and the voluntary and community sector set out how they should work together.[4] Many local authorities subsequently developed Local Compacts with the third sector in their area, modelled on the national Compact. Problems continued, however, and proposals for an additional Compact Plus scheme were published for consultation in March 2005.

---

1    For a discussion of Third Sector characteristics, see 'Exploring the role of the third sector in public service delivery and reform: a discussion document' published by HM Treasury, February 2005.
2    A glossary of terms used is provided in Appendix 2 of this report.
3    Estimates of the amount of government funding to the third sector are discussed in Part 1 of this report. These estimates exclude work done by unpaid volunteers, which some estimates value at around £40 billion per year, some 20 times the amount of public funding.
4    'The Compact on relations between the government and the voluntary and community sector' Home Office 1998, available to download from www. thecompact.org.uk.

**1** Some examples of third sector organisations which provide public services

**The Prince's Trust** is a national charity which works with disadvantaged young people aged between 14 and 30, providing personal development support, business start-up loans and other services such as support for ex-offenders. The Prince's Trust has a turnover of around £50 million per year. It receives a mix of public and private funding, including funding from most government departments at national, regional and local levels.

**The Family Welfare Association**, based in East London, provides a variety of services to support families, including mental health services, residential care, day centres, marriage and family support services. Of its annual turnover of £12.5 million, £11 million comes from contracts and grants from various government sources, including Sure Start, the Children's Fund, Connexions and funding from the local Primary Care Trust. The remaining £1.5 million comes from fund-raising.

**DIAL Shropshire Telford and Wrekin**, part of national charity DIAL UK, provides disability advice services in Shropshire. It has offices in Shrewsbury and Telford and a team of 45 volunteers. The charity provides information and advice on disability issues, as well as supporting its clients to apply for appropriate benefits and to challenge benefits applications which are rejected. More than 50 per cent of its £200,000 annual turnover comes from Learning and Skills Council funding for two projects. Other significant funders include the Legal Services Commission (£12,000) and Telford and Wrekin District Council (£13,000).

*Source: National Audit Office*

**5**    Funding processes have been a particular stumbling-block, despite the existence of a Compact code of practice on funding.[5] In 2002, a Treasury Review of the involvement of the sector in public services[6] identified several important and commonplace weaknesses in funding processes and made recommendations for improvement. This report examines the progress made by departments and other government funders, led by the Home Office, on improving the way they fund the sector to deliver public services.

**6**    The Treasury 2002 review provided a good framework for better use of TSOs in the delivery of public services. Successful implementation is, however, dependent on departments' willingness to embrace new ways of working and to embed new practices across their funding streams. Our work takes those efforts further forward, by encouraging greater co-ordination amongst civil servants responsible for such activities, dissemination of good practice, and training and support for those involved, including encouraging a degree of specialisation in procuring and funding services from TSOs. We also identified a need for greater clarity and guidance on some of the principles promulgated by the 2002 review, for example on full cost recovery, through mechanisms such as worked case examples. Where departments are in effect procuring a service from TSOs, it may be more appropriate to engage with TSOs on the same basis as when services are procured from the private sector.

**7**    Recent work to examine the efficiency of the public sector as a whole has re-emphasised the importance of effective working with the third sector. Sir Peter Gershon's 2004 Efficiency Review[7] recommended that government should adopt four key principles for third sector funding – longer-term funding, appropriate balance of risk between the funder and the TSO, full cost recovery and streamlined monitoring and reporting – reflecting the key concerns of the Compact and the Treasury Review. These principles promote efficiency in public funding – for example, longer-term contracts mean TSOs can retain staff and make investments to improve services – and apply equally to public procurement from small and medium-sized private companies.

**8**    Our work is based principally on a review of the practices, policies and progress made by central government departments. We also held a number of group discussions, workshops and individual interviews, both with funders and TSOs, to explore specific issues and case examples. We worked in partnership with the National Council for Voluntary Organisations (NCVO). NCVO's research team carried out the bulk of the research to examine the sector's perspective on progress on funding issues. We are grateful to NCVO for their assistance.

---

5    Originally published in 2000, the Compact funding code was revised in March 2005. The new Compact Code of Good Practice on Funding and Procurement is available to download from www.thecompact.org.uk.

6    *'The role of the voluntary and community sector in service delivery: a cross cutting review'* published by HM Treasury 2002.

7    *'Releasing Resources for the Frontline: Independent Review of Public Sector Efficiency'*, HM Treasury July 2004.

# Key findings and conclusions

**9**    Our work has focused on the action taken by government departments to improve their funding relationships with TSOs; however, the third sector itself also has a responsibility to take an active part. The National Council for Voluntary Organisations, our partner in this research, has published its own report which complements this report and a summary of its recommendations is given at the end of this Summary. The Association of Chief Executives of Voluntary Organisations is also active in promoting a better relationship between government and the sector, principally through its 'Surer Funding' report.[8]

## At a strategic level

**10    Data on the sector and its part in delivering public services needs to be improved.** The Home Office has a target to increase the sector's involvement in public services by 5 per cent, by 2006. There appears to be an upward trend in the amount of government funding provided to the sector, but the Home Office's estimates of the funding distributed by government differ from estimates made by the voluntary sector of funding which it receives from government sources. This discrepancy appears to have several causes, including the different ways in which the sector and 'public services' can be defined, limitations of departments' information systems and the complexity of central and local government's funding relationships with the sector. More reliable and timely data are needed, to gauge the sector's contribution to public services and to understand whether it is growing as government intends. The Home Office is currently working to develop a standard information requirement for government bodies, which it expects will improve the quality of the information provided.

**11    Despite the lead provided by the Home Office and the Treasury, departments need to develop their capacity to work better with the sector.** All major funding departments have both senior "champions" and middle-ranking liaison officers with specific responsibility for encouraging implementation of the Treasury Review.

During 2004 and early 2005 most departments produced a strategy outlining their future plans to further involve the sector in their areas of responsibility. The development of these strategies often involved contributions from departments' finance and procurement specialists, who advise staff who are responsible for awarding funds to TSOs. However, in most cases these strategies are at an early stage of implementation. In the absence of such a strategy, departments have to date relied mostly on individual initiative to improve funding practices, rather than developing expertise across their organisations. In addition, apart from a few high-profile initiatives there is little evidence of effective joint working across Whitehall.

**12    The recommendations of the Cross-Cutting Review have been addressed, but further steps are needed to improve funding in practice.** More needs to be done to translate high-level commitments into practical results wherever government interacts with TSOs, and to introduce additional mechanisms for improving funding practice. Our research shows that most TSOs have not seen any general improvement in funding practices since 2002, and in some cases funding practices are perceived to have worsened.

**13    Spreading good funding practice throughout government and at local level is a particular challenge.** Much of the funding for TSOs passes through executive agencies and Non-Departmental Public Bodies (NDPBs), regional bodies and local authorities; for these bodies, as for departments, good funding practices are not yet the norm. Indeed, the National Audit Office believes that the complexities and transaction costs of filtering money through a variety of organisations until it reaches the front line should be simplified and reduced wherever possible. Some intermediary bodies appreciate and have adopted the Treasury's recommendations, but others, particularly those where an effective relationship with the sector is not perceived as central to their work, have not yet taken these recommendations on board. Our research suggests that funding problems are particularly acute at local level, despite the adoption of Local Compacts by many local authorities.[9]

---

8    *'Surer Funding'*, ACEVO Commission of Inquiry Report, ACEVO November 2004.
9    At the time of writing this report, 278 of the 388 local authorities in England (71 per cent) had published a Local Compact and a further 100 were planning to do so (source: Compact Working Group).

## At an operational level

**14    Funders need to be clearer about the purpose of funding, and decide for each funding programme whether they are engaged in supporting a worthy cause ('giving'), procuring services ('shopping') or in building capacity in the sector ('investing').**[10] Each purpose requires a different approach, with 'shopping' being the most appropriate model for the delivery of public services. The 'shopping' approach to funding implies a need for a tightly-specified contract and procurement processes, while 'investing' and 'giving' approaches are closer to conventional grant-making. Currently there is little settled practice on whether to use grants or contracts, and both funding models are often inappropriately used. Potential conflicts with European Union rules on state aid must also be considered.[11]

**15    There has been little progress on reimbursing the full costs of service delivery or the associated question of whether funding should be given as a grant award or a contract after procurement.** The two issues are closely connected, since 'grant' funding often requires TSOs to detail precisely what costs the grant will cover. Most contracts for service delivery, at least when agreed with private sector suppliers, focus on the price bid by the supplier and on the desired outcome, not on details of the supplier's costs. Many TSOs complain that government funders are inconsistent in their treatment of TSO suppliers, too often relying on a grant culture and thus requiring a much greater level of cost disclosure than they would expect of private sector firms. Existing guidance to funders has touched on these issues but has tended to focus on principles rather than practice, leaving practitioners unclear as to how to take this forward. There is much that could be learned and applied from good procurement practice, especially the work done by the Office of Government Commerce in relation to procurement involving the small and medium-size enterprises with whom many TSOs share many characteristics. Meanwhile, TSOs and their representative organisations have a parallel responsibility to develop their understanding of their cost structures and to use the information to inform their applications for funding.

**16    There is still plenty of scope for moving to longer-term funding and away from annual awards.** The 2002 Treasury Review identified that TSOs were too often reliant on annual funding which made it difficult to provide continuity of service and certainty of funding, causing avoidable costs for the TSOs (and funders) concerned, especially when award decisions were delayed. And this uncertainty can cut into the quality of work that the TSO does by diverting staff away from front-line duties. There have been some encouraging developments since 2002, but annual funding remains the norm, especially at local level, although future changes to local authority funding are expected to facilitate longer-term funding arrangements with TSOs. The National Audit Office believes that this in part reflects a general suspicion and lack of trust together with a tendency to underrate the sector's professionalism and ability to deliver public services. Without trust, partnerships cannot work. Government funders have much more to do therefore to 'mainstream' the sector into public service delivery and thereby secure the full contribution which the third sector can provide.

**17    Funders have made better progress in streamlining application processes and moving to funding in advance of expenditure.** Most departments have been able to make helpful changes to application processes for at least some of their funding, through means such as two-stage application processes, use of online application forms and funding portals on the internet. Departments have shown a greater willingness to make payments in advance of expenditure, for example through profile (or instalment) funding, following the issue of new Treasury guidance, to ease the financing burden on TSOs.

**18    There has been less success in reducing the burden of monitoring.** A pilot to examine the scope for sharing information between funders had some success in reducing the burden of administration involved in making funding awards. But the pilot was much less successful in reducing the burden of monitoring which TSOs face. Although funders have made various efforts to improve monitoring systems, the impact of these changes has not been widely felt and there is still a need for monitoring systems which are proportionate to the risks, the amounts of funding and the nature of the service involved.

---

10    Concept taken from *'The Grant-making Tango: Issues for Funders'* by Julia Unwin, published by the Baring Foundation 2004.
11    The Office of Government Commerce points out that government provision of equipment or space for a TSO might qualify as inappropriate state aid if this support provides the TSO with a financial cushion allowing it to bid for a public contract.

# RECOMMENDATIONS

**19** The specific recommendations of the 2002 Treasury Review have in the main been implemented (as shown in Appendix 1 of this report), but this has not yet been enough to bring about a widespread and substantive change in departments' funding practices. Whilst the Home Office and the Treasury have sought to move matters forward, a significant gap remains between the principles set out in the Treasury Review and subsequent practice. Our recommendations focus on how best to fill that gap.

**20** The **Home Office**, as the government department with lead responsibility for these issues, the Treasury and other government departments should work together to:

1 **Improve information about the sector's involvement in public services,** by collaborating with other expert organisations to strengthen national and local data on the amounts of public sector funding going to the sector. Funders should introduce systems to clearly distinguish payments to TSOs from other spending, enabling data on their TSO funding to be collated quickly;

2 **Introduce new measures to improve funding practices, including:**

   a   issuing a checklist of good funding practice, as a simple reference point for both funders and providers – as the Home Office now proposes;[12]

   b   identifying and promoting 'beacon[13]' funders at all levels of government, to act as centres of expertise and help spread good practice;

   c   establishing an annual awards scheme to recognise and celebrate good practice and innovation in the way funders and third sector providers work together for successful service delivery;

   d   making all relevant guidance to government funders, whether produced by government or outside experts, available from a single source to provide a web-based 'virtual university' for funders;

   e   considering the potential benefits of an accreditation process to 'kitemark' funders complying with the principles of the Treasury Review, and bring forward recommendations on this; and

   f   supporting other government departments in implementing the measures recommended below.

---

12   The Home Office's proposals for 'Compact Plus' outlined in paragraph 21 of this report, include a checklist of good funding practice. 'Effective Local Partnerships', a checklist for local funders and third sector organisations, was published by the Treasury in February 2005, as part of the results of the Treasury's Voluntary and Community Sector Review 2004. Meanwhile, the ACEVO report 'Surer Funding' published in November 2004, proposes a checklist of good funding practice.

13   This recommendation is inspired by the Beacon Councils scheme operated by IDeA, the improvement and development agency for local government. The scheme identifies local authorities with expertise in specific policy areas and helps them to share good practice with other local authorities.

3 **Develop targeted guidance on those funding issues which cause most difficulty**, working in collaboration with the Office of Government Commerce (OGC). There is already a variety of funding guidance in existence covering general funding principles; new material should focus on adding value for funders in their everyday work. It might cover, for example, guidelines on whether and when to use grants, contracts and procurement processes; grant terms and conditions which run counter to good value for money; contractual elements which are unhelpful; and how and when to apply the principle of full cost recovery. The latter would complement the guidance produced for the sector by the Association of Chief Executives of Voluntary Organisations (ACEVO). The NAO would be pleased to work with the Home Office and other key stakeholders on developing new guidance;

4 **Establish a champion or panel of experts** to advise on funding practice, when approached following discussions between TSOs and their funders. In procurement situations, competition and procurement laws should apply;

5 **Expand the scope of the government funding web-based portal within an agreed timescale**, to include details of all government grant funding which is available to the sector;

6 **Designate and train individuals and groups of staff to specialise in working with the sector**, including working with procurement methods and experts where this is appropriate, focusing training on the funding issues which cause most difficulty and providing opportunities for staff to undertake secondments to TSOs;

7 **Expand the role of departmental champions and liaison officers** – in addition to their intra-departmental role – to include regular contact with third sector providers and groups of providers, where this does not already occur;

8 **Develop Gershon-style joint or shared teams** for dealing with funding third sector service providers, especially where individual funders are not large enough to provide a critical mass to maintain such expertise alone;

9 **Develop a template contract** for procurement from the third sector, suitable for adapting to special requirements;

# RECOMMENDATIONS (continued)

10 **Fully integrate, where appropriate, their associated executive agencies and Non-Departmental Public Bodies** into departmental strategies for working with TSOs;

11 **Commission further research into local funding practices,** leading to recommendations for improvement at a local level. Key stakeholders such as the Office of the Deputy Prime Minister (ODPM), the local government improvement agency IDeA, the Audit Commission and the Local Government Association should be involved in this research. The research could also extend to other local funders including regional bodies and local health organisations;

12 **Above all, seek through training and co-operation, greater trust between the governmental authorities and the third sector** so that real partnership can be created and inform the relationships between funding and service suppliers.

21 In March 2005 the Home Office published proposals for a new Compact Plus scheme, which public sector bodies and TSOs will be able to opt into if they wish. The proposals, which are undergoing consultation until 12 July 2005, are in part informed by our review and our discussions with the Home Office. The proposals directly address some of our recommendations, for example by putting forward a list of good funding practices and a 'kitemark' for members of the scheme. The Home Office proposals also suggest that a 'Compact Champion' should be established who would be independent of both the sector and government. This proposal is in line with our recommendation above. Further details of the Home Office proposals are given in the main text of this report.

22 **Internal and external auditors should work with funders and sector representatives to produce guidance on the monitoring and audit processes best suited to different types and values of funding.** Monitoring processes should be proportionate – tailored to the amount of funding, good financial management and risk to value for money in specific cases. This work should build on the 'lead funder' and 'Combined Audit National Pilot' projects described later in this report, and address funders' reluctance to share information and assurance about TSOs they fund jointly. The National Audit Office would be happy to contribute to this work.

**23**   Improvements to funding practice require the active involvement of **TSOs** as well as funders. For example, an effective approach to full cost recovery requires that TSOs have a good understanding of their cost structure, which they use to inform their bids for public service contracts. The third sector will also need to make changes to the way it works. The National Council for Voluntary Organisations published its own report[14] on the funding relationship with government, in June 2005. Its key recommendations include:

■   **Full cost recovery** – TSOs must own the principle of full cost recovery, ensure that they cost contract bids appropriately and consider refusing to accept under-funded contracts;

■   **Sustainable funding environment** – TSOs should seek clarity about the length of funding they are bidding for, improve their skills and knowledge about different funding mechanisms, and take on responsibility for their own sustainability in the long term;

■   **Application processes** – TSOs need to improve their skills base in making applications, help to reduce the administrative burden and always request feedback from funders;

■   **Relationships with funders** – TSOs should work with funders to design targets, outcomes and mechanisms for monitoring and evaluation;

■   **Delivery through tiers of government** – local funders and local TSOs should explore ways that they can work together to ensure that public services are adequately resourced.

**24**   Meanwhile, the Association of Chief Executives of Voluntary Organisations feels that many TSOs need to develop their skills in analysing their costs and negotiating contracts with public funders. Its report *'Surer Funding'*, showed that current contracts between government and the sector are failing to deliver value for money. The Association is working to encourage TSOs to adopt its template for analysing and allocating overhead costs[15] and to encourage the adoption of its Surer Funding framework across government.

**25**   Third sector representative bodies, including the National Council for Voluntary Organisations and the Association of Chief Executives of Voluntary Organisations, are working to improve the sector's skills in negotiating contracts, through the 'finance hub' being set up as part of the Home Office's ChangeUp initiative (see paragraph 2.2 of this report). The finance hub is led by the Charities Aid Foundation.

14    *'Shared aspirations: the role of the voluntary and community sector in improving the funding relationships with government'*, NCVO June 2005.
15    *'Full Cost Recovery: a guide and toolkit on cost allocation'*, ACEVO/New Philanthropy Capital 2004.

# PART ONE
## Introduction

**1.1** This report examines how government departments and other funders can best work with the third sector to improve their funding relationship, achieving better value for money in public services. This part of our report describes the sector and the role it plays in public services. It also sets out some recent initiatives to increase the sector's role, and the attention given to improving the way government funds the sector to deliver public services.

# The third sector is a significant contributor to national life and public services

**1.2** The third sector is the term used to describe the range of organisations which are neither state nor the private sector. Third sector organisations (TSOs) include small local community organisations, and large, established, national and international voluntary or charitable organisations. Some rely solely on the efforts of volunteers; others employ paid professional staff and have management structures and processes similar to those of businesses, large or small; many are registered charities whilst others operate as co-operatives, "social enterprises" or companies limited by guarantee. **Figure 2** provides more information about the types of organisations in the third sector. All share some common characteristics in the social, environmental or cultural objectives they pursue; their independence from government; and the reinvestment of surpluses for those same objectives.[16]

---

**2**    Types of organisations in the third sector

**Voluntary and community sector**
Includes registered charities, as well as non-charitable non-profit organisations, associations, self-help groups and community groups. Most involve some aspect of voluntary activity, though many are also professional organisations with paid staff. 'Community organisations' tend to be focused on particular localities or groups within the community; many are dependent entirely or almost entirely on voluntary activity.

**General charities**
Charities registered with the Charity Commission except those considered part of the government apparatus, such as universities, and those financial institutions considered part of the corporate sector.

**Social enterprise**
A business with primarily social objectives whose surpluses are principally reinvested for that purpose in the business or community, rather than being driven by the need to maximise profit for shareholders and owners.

**Mutuals and co-operatives**
Membership-based organisations run on a democratic basis for the benefit of their members. Members may be their employees or their consumers or be drawn from the wider community. Some employee co-operatives may be essentially private businesses but many mutuals and co-operatives consider themselves part of the social enterprise sector.

*Source: NCVO and the Treasury*

NOTE
Many organisations fall into more than one of the categories above.

---

16    For a discussion of the characteristics of the third sector, see *'Exploring the Third Sector in Public Service Delivery and Reform: A Discussion Document,'* HM Treasury, February 2005.

**1.3** There are no reliable figures on the economic activity of the sector as a whole. There were more than 166,000 registered charities in the UK in September 2004 with a total income of £34.6 billion in 2003-04. In addition there are many TSOs which are not registered.[17] According to some estimates there may be as many as 500,000 TSOs in the UK. Around 70 per cent of TSOs operate at local level. Unpaid volunteers carry out much of the work done by TSOs; some estimates value the contribution of volunteers to the UK economy in tens of billions of pounds.

**1.4** The sector is involved in many areas of public service delivery (**Figure 3**). The concentration of third sector funding in a few major departments (**Figure 4**) reflects the policy areas in which TSOs have traditionally been involved: crime prevention and reduction, health and social services, community transport, the arts and sport, education, overseas development and community regeneration.[18] But the sector is also involved in less obvious areas such as veterans' services, advice on tax, and national procurement strategies at the Department of Health.

| **3** Examples of programmes involving the third sector | |
|---|---|
| **Home Office** | Crime prevention/management programmes |
| | Drug Action Teams – local co-ordinating groups set up under the government's national drugs strategy |
| | Victim Support – national charity providing support and information for victims of crime |
| **Department for Education and Skills** | Children's Fund – services for disadvantaged children and young people aged 5 to 13 |
| | Safeguarding Children and Supporting Families Grants – children's social care |
| | Sure Start – childcare, health and emotional development services for young children |
| | Connexions – information and advice for young people aged 13 to 19 |
| **Office of the Deputy Prime Minister** | New Deal for Communities – alleviating deprivation in the most disadvantaged communities |
| | Homelessness and hostel provision |
| **Department for Work and Pensions** | New Deal for Young People – employment advice and help for young people aged 18 to 24 |
| **Department for Transport** | Funding for transport services in rural areas and for disadvantaged groups, such as the Rural Bus Subsidy Grant and the Rural and Urban Bus Challenge Grant |
| **Department of Health and National Health Service** | Funding for charity-run hospices |
| | Digital hearing aids provided through partnership with RNID (Royal National Institute for the Deaf) |
| | Variety of health services such as care for cancer patients (e.g. Marie Curie Cancer Care) |
| **Ministry of Defence** | Veterans' services such as housing and employment advice, rehabilitation for war pensioners |
| | Skill Force – vocational training for young people aged 14 to 16 |
| **HM Revenue and Customs** | Pilot schemes offering advice on eligibility for tax credits |

*Source: National Audit Office*

NOTE

This table is not intended to provide a comprehensive list of government programmes involving the third sector, but an indication of the range of activities in which TSOs are involved. Some significant third sector funders (e.g. the Department for Environment, Food and Rural Affairs) are not included here.

17 Charities which have an annual income of less than £1,000, do not have the use of land or buildings and do not have any permanent endowments, do not have to register. Also, to be defined as a charity an organisation must be set up exclusively for charitable purposes (defined in charity law to include the relief of financial hardship, the advancement of education, the advancement of religion and certain other purposes), for the public benefit.

18 The most recent data available, for 2001-02, do not take account of changes to the structure of government since then, particularly the establishment of the Office of the Deputy Prime Minister (ODPM) and the Department for Transport. ODPM can help to promote good practice in the funding of TSOs by local authorities.

## 4 Distribution of third sector funding by department, in 2000-01 and 2001-02

A few departments control most of central government's third sector funding

Chart: horizontal bar chart showing Funding to TSOs (£ million) by department, comparing 2001-02 and 2000-01.

Departments (top to bottom): HO, DCMS, DfEE/DfES, DTI, DfID, LCD/DCA, MAFF/Defra, DoH, MoD, DETR/DTLR, FCO, CO, IR, DSS/DWP

Annotations: 2001-02, 2000-01, (£1.02 billion total), (£998 million total), (+ funding to housing associations)

X-axis: Funding to TSOs (£ million) — 0, 50, 100, 150, 200, 250, 300, 350, 400

*Source: Home Office, 'Central Government Funding of Voluntary and Community Organisations, 1982-83 to 2001-02'*

NOTES

The Figure does not reflect subsequent changes in government – MAFF, the former Ministry of Agriculture, Fisheries and Food, became part of the Department for Environment, Food and Rural Affairs (Defra). DETR/DTLR is the former Department of the Environment, Transport and the Regions (DETR), which became the Department for Transport, Local Government and the Regions (DTLR), and (since the date of this chart) the Department for Transport (DfT) and the Office of the Deputy Prime Minister (ODPM).

DCMS (Department for Culture, Media and Sport) funding does not include Lottery funding. Most DCMS funding is distributed by non-departmental public bodies such as Arts Council England, rather than directly by the Department.

Department of Trade and Industry (DTI) data reflect the Department's assumption of responsibility for the Regional Development Agencies, including Single Regeneration Budget funding associated with the former Department for the Environment, Transport and the Regions (DETR) and its successor, the Department for Transport, Local Government and the Regions (DTLR).

DoH funding does not include National Health Service (NHS) spending.

The chart includes (in the DETR/DTLR bars) an indication of how the funding distribution changes if funds provided to housing associations are included. The scope of this report has not included housing associations, but they are included in the data that the Home Office gathers on third sector funding.

DWP appears from this chart to have no funding relationships with TSOs, since at the time this data was produced, contracts with TSOs for employment services (now managed by DWP) were the responsibility of the former Department for Education and Employment (DfEE).

The chart includes funding provided through departments' associated executive agencies and non-departmental public bodies (such as the Commission for Racial Equality, the Probation Service and the Youth Justice Board in the case of the Home Office).

This chart does not include 'indirect' public funding from sources such as Gift Aid in the tax system.

In some cases (including funding for the arts, sport, agriculture, housing and crime prevention), the figures given are for spending in England only – additional sums are distributed by the National Assembly for Wales, the Northern Ireland Executive and the Scottish Executive. In other areas figures for spending on TSOs in the whole of the UK are given since figures for England alone are not available.

## The relationship between government and the sector has not always been effective

**1.5** Despite the sector's important and growing role in public services, the relationship between government and the sector has suffered from a variety of problems. According to the Treasury Review of 2002, the sector often felt that it was not being engaged as a partner by government, and was not asked to contribute to the design of policy. Some TSOs readily embraced a role in public service delivery, whilst others wished to avoid too close a connection with government for fear of reducing their independence or ability to campaign. The Review also concluded that the sector generally lacked management capacity, which limited its ability to bid for and deliver contracts for public services, particularly when in competition with the private sector.

**1.6** There were a series of initiatives by both government and the sector to improve their relationship. In 1996, the Deakin Commission Report[19] charted a way forward for the sector. The Report contributed to the establishment in 1998 of the Compact, which set out how the government and the sector should work together. A series of Compact Codes of Good Practice covered specific aspects of government-sector joint working, such as policy appraisal, working with black and minority ethnic (BME) groups and volunteering. Many local authorities and Local Strategic Partnerships[20] drew up 'Local Compacts' with TSOs in their areas.

**1.7** Despite all this, many TSOs criticised the implementation of the Compact, saying that many funders were either unaware of it or did not put its principles into practice. Funding practices have underlain many of the difficulties in the relationship between government and the sector. A code of good practice on funding which was published in 2000, in association with the 1998 Compact, was updated to include procurement and reissued in March 2005.[21]

## The 2002 Treasury Spending Review sought to tackle the issue

**1.8** The September 2002 Treasury Cross-Cutting Review *'The Role of the Voluntary and Community Sector in Service Delivery'*, conducted and published as part of the 2002 Spending Review, looked again at the relationship between government and the sector. It sought to remedy the implementation problems which had affected the Compact, and looked at building capacity within the sector and improving the way government funds the sector. The Review made over 40 recommendations to government departments and the sector, which the government expects to see implemented in full by April 2006. There were 14 recommendations related to funding (**see Figure 5** and Appendix 1 for the full wording of the recommendations). The Review covered England only.

| **5** | Funding and related recommendations from the 2002 Treasury Review |
|---|---|

| Recommendations | Coverage |
|---|---|
| 12 | Improvements to data on government funding of the sector |
| 13-16 | Encouraging full cost recovery (reimbursement of overheads as well as direct project costs) |
| 17-18 | Streamlining access and performance management requirements for multiple, often small, funding streams |
| 19-20 | Reducing end loading of payments (payment in arrears) |
| 21-22 | Achieving a more stable funding relationship |
| 27-29 | Implementation of the Compact |

*Source: National Audit Office*

---

19 *'Meeting the Challenge of Change: Voluntary Action into the 21st Century'*, NCVO 1996. Produced by the Commission on the Future of the Voluntary Sector, chaired by Nicholas Deakin and set up by NCVO.

20 Local Strategic Partnerships bring together public, private and third sector organisations within the area covered by a particular local authority. 88 LSPs in the most deprived areas of England receive extra funding through the Neighbourhood Renewal Fund.

21 See footnote 5 on page 2 of this report.

# There is a government-wide target for increasing the role of the sector

**1.9**  The Home Office, which is responsible for policy relating to the third sector, is also responsible for leading other government departments in their implementation of the recommendations of the 2002 review. It also has a Public Service Agreement (PSA) target to achieve a 5 per cent increase in the volume of public services provided through the sector by 2006. The Department measures progress against this target through a survey of 4,482 TSOs throughout England, of a range of sizes and types. As yet only one set of data, for the financial year 2002-03, has been collected. The Home Office published provisional findings based on this data in late 2004 and expects to publish a full report in summer 2005. It is currently collecting data for 2003-04 and anticipates that comparative data will be available in late autumn 2005. It is therefore not yet possible to report on progress towards the target.

**1.10**  The Home Office estimates that central government funding of TSOs, excluding housing associations, in the UK was £2.03 billion (£3.32 billion including housing associations)[22] in the financial year 2001-02, the most recent year for which data is available. As **Figure 6** shows, funding has been increasing in recent years; in the two years before 2001-02 it rose by 43 per cent and 37 per cent (23 per cent and 21 per cent including housing associations). However, this increase occurred from a relatively low base, after a long period of decline. And this total still represents a small proportion of all central government spending, at around 0.5 per cent.[23]

**1.11**  In addition to central government funding, other public funders also provide significant funding to TSOs. The Home Office estimates that in 2001-02, government funding of TSOs totalled £5.08 billion (£6.37 billion including housing association spending), of which £2.03 billion (£3.32 billion including housing associations) came from central government; £1.87 billion from local authorities; £904 million from the National Health Service and £274 million from the European Union.[24]

**1.12**  The Home Office's figure for total funding differs from the estimate made by the sector itself of the funding it receives. The National Council for Voluntary Organisations (NCVO) estimates that the sector received £7.14 billion in public sector funding in 2001-02, some 12 per cent more than the Home Office estimate of £6.37 billion. The Home Office and NCVO suggest that the reasons for the discrepancy include:

- variable quality of data collected by government bodies, which often do not clearly identify funding to TSOs in their record-keeping;

- variable quality of data provided by TSOs on funding received;

- differences in the scope of data collection:

  - the Home Office collects information on "voluntary/community organisations" broadly defined, including organisations registered with the Charity Commission and those not registered. NCVO has its own definition of "general charities" as "private, non-profit-making bodies serving persons";

  - the Home Office and NCVO have different rules for including or excluding funding from certain types of organisations. For example, the Home Office includes funding of housing associations and excludes National Lottery funding and funding provided by foreign countries, while NCVO excludes funding of housing associations and includes National Lottery funding and funding provided by foreign countries;

- differences in the methodology of data collection – the Home Office collects information from government bodies and reports the figures provided, while NCVO analyses the annual accounts of a sample of organisations and uses this sample to make an estimate for the sector as a whole.

22    Home Office estimate at current prices.
23    If housing association spending is included the figure rises to around 1 per cent.
24    The sector also receives funding from the National Lottery, £550 million in 2001-02 (source: NCVO), but this is excluded from Home Office data.

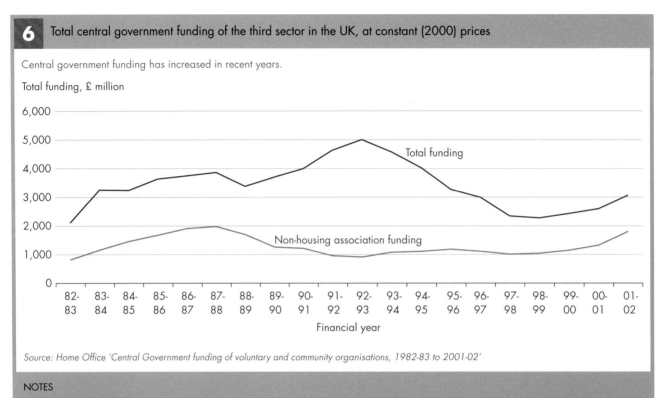

**6** Total central government funding of the third sector in the UK, at constant (2000) prices

Central government funding has increased in recent years.

Total funding, £ million

Total funding

Non-housing association funding

Financial year

Source: Home Office 'Central Government funding of voluntary and community organisations, 1982-83 to 2001-02'

NOTES

The peak in funding in 1987-88 is mainly due to measures to regenerate inner cities and combat high unemployment, such as the Manpower Services Commission's £564 million funding of the Community Programme in 1987-88.

The data in this chart for 2001-02 does not exactly match the figures quoted in paragraph 1.11, since the chart is based on estimates at constant (2000) prices, while the figures quoted in paragraph 1.11 are the Home Office's estimates at current prices, as this report was produced.

## The Home Office works with others to implement the Compact and the 2002 Review's recommendations

**1.13** The Home Office works closely with the Treasury, which co-ordinates spending reviews and the cross-cutting reviews of the third sector's involvement in public services.[25] Within the Home Office, the Active Communities Directorate is responsible for relations with the sector and for overseeing implementation of the Treasury Review recommendations.

**1.14** The Home Office also co-ordinates a working group including 'Grade 3 Champions' (senior civil servants) from the largest funding departments, voluntary sector organisations and other stakeholders such as the Local Government Association. The Home Office and the Treasury have both produced a variety of guidance for departments on implementing the Treasury Review recommendations, including Home Office guidance on procurement of services from the sector,[26] and Treasury guidance to funders.[27]

**1.15** Implementation in other government departments is assisted by the Grade 3 Champions and their Voluntary and Community Sector Liaison Officers, more junior civil servants. Both Grade 3 Champions and Voluntary and Community Sector Liaison Officers meet regularly to report on progress and share experiences. They are responsible for drawing up departmental strategies for engaging with the sector, most of which were submitted to the Home Office during 2004.

**1.16** Government departments are also responsible for encouraging their associated public bodies, such as executive agencies, to implement the Treasury Review's recommendations. Executive agencies and Government Offices for the Regions were both included in the scope of the national Compact. Non-departmental public bodies (NDPBs) were not included, although the Compact states that the government would actively encourage the extension of the Compact to include them.

25    The 2002 Treasury Review, which this report takes as its starting point, was followed by a further review of the role of the third sector, as part of the Treasury's 2004 Spending Review.
26    'Think Smart…Think Voluntary Sector! Good practice guidance on procurement of services from the Voluntary and Community Sector', Home Office 2004.
27    'Guidance to Funders: Improving funding relationships for voluntary and community organisations', HM Treasury 2003.

**1.17** The National Council for Voluntary Organisations (NCVO), as a membership organisation representing the sector, monitors and encourages the development of the national Compact and Local Compacts, hosting the Compact Working Group and running the Compact Advocacy Programme which aims to highlight and resolve breaches of the national Compact. NCVO also carries out a range of work to promote government and the third sector's understanding of the sector's role in public service delivery, such as published case studies, reports[28] and conferences.

**1.18** The Association of Chief Executives of Voluntary Organisations (ACEVO) has also been active in the area of voluntary sector funding, providing guidance to TSOs on cost allocation. An ACEVO Commission of Inquiry carried out a recent review on how to encourage "surer funding" for TSOs.[29] The review illustrated how poor funding relationships can waste public money through loading excessive risk onto the TSO providers. For example, Marie Curie Cancer Care provides nursing services for people dying from cancer, under contracts with Primary Care Trusts. However, the contracts are structured so that the inevitable uncertainty in demand for nursing services is borne entirely by Marie Curie Cancer Care, not by the Primary Care Trusts. The ultimate effect is that emergency admissions to hospital increase, raising overall costs for the PCT.

## The Home Office has recently proposed a new approach

**1.19** In March 2005 the Home Office published proposals for a Compact Plus scheme, which public sector bodies and TSOs will be able to opt into if they wish. The proposals include:

- a 'kitemark' for organisations signing up to Compact Plus, for display on their publicity material;

- a Compact Champion, independent of both government and the sector, who would review organisations' adherence to the Compact Plus principles, and adjudicate in disputes.

**1.20** The Compact Plus proposals on funding would go beyond the Compact and the Treasury Review by turning recommended funding practices into commitments with associated sanctions (removal of the proposed kitemark, and possibly financial penalties awarded by the Compact Champion), for organisations opting into the scheme.

Most of the funding proposals – minimising bureaucracy in funding applications and audit requirements, multi-year funding and funding for overhead costs – reinforce principles from the Compact and the Treasury Review. One new proposal suggests that public sector bodies should use procurement rather than grants when seeking to deliver public services through the third sector and should not ask for information about management fees and overheads. This aims to enable TSOs to compete on equal terms with private sector suppliers.

**1.21** The Compact Plus proposals are under consultation until 12 July 2005, after which the Home Office will bring forward revised proposals.

## This report covers the full range of government bodies involved in funding the sector

**1.22** This report focuses on central government's progress in implementing the recommendations of the Treasury Review, including action taken by central government departments, NDPBs and executive agencies and Government Offices for the Regions. We have also undertaken a more limited evaluation of local government funding practices. Our report covers:

- funders' capacity to work with the sector (Part 2);

- the development of better funding methods (Part 3); and

- efforts to streamline application and monitoring processes (Part 4).

**1.23** Our principal source of evidence has been a review of the practices, policies and progress made by central government departments. In addition we held a number of group discussions, workshops and individual interviews, both with funders and TSOs, to explore specific issues and case examples. We reviewed a large amount of supporting documentation and corroborated our findings with the TSOs concerned. We also worked in partnership with NCVO. Its research team carried out the bulk of our research with the sector, including TSOs' views on funding developments. We are grateful to NCVO for their support and co-operation during our review. Further details of our methodology are given in Appendix 3. A full glossary is at Appendix 2.

---

28     For example, 'The Reform of Public Services: the role of the voluntary sector', NCVO, May 2005.
29     'Surer Funding' ACEVO Commission of Inquiry Report, November 2004.

## PART TWO
# Funders can do more to improve their capacity to work with the sector

**2.1** Improvements in departments' funding practices depend on the skill of those officials who design and manage funding relationships. The expertise of programme managers, finance staff and procurement departments is vital if high-level commitments are to be translated into better funding practice. This Part of the report examines the progress departments are making in developing their capacity to work with the sector for better value for money.

## Some recent initiatives aim to strengthen the sector's capacity to deliver public services

**2.2** Since 2002 a number of initiatives have been launched to increase the sector's capacity to deliver public services:

- **ChangeUp**, a Home Office strategy aimed at improving support and infrastructure for TSOs. ChangeUp includes plans for a national hub of expertise on financing TSO activity, which is expected to be established during 2005 along with five other hubs covering expertise in performance improvement, workforce development, governance, ICT and recruitment and developing volunteers. Regional delivery of ChangeUp is managed by the Government Offices for the Regions. By 2006, local plans for TSO support are expected to be in place.

The initiative provides £150 million in funding, spread over four financial years from 2004-05 to 2007-08. From 2006-07 it will be managed by a new organisation led by the third sector, to be known as Capacity Builders.

- **Futurebuilders**, a £215 million fund from the Home Office, providing mainly loans and some grants for TSOs involved in public service delivery. The first round of Futurebuilders applications was processed during 2004 and the first award decisions were announced in February 2005. The fund is intended to address the limitations of the conventional capital markets in lending to TSOs, by providing investment finance for service delivery. Futurebuilders funding will be provided on a longer-term basis than most grant funding.

- **The Capital Programme**, a £4 million fund which will provide loans for small and start-up TSOs to obtain workspaces;

- **The Treasury Spending Review 2004** included reviews of five key policy areas, with the aim of identifying ways in which the sector's involvement in departmental programmes could be strengthened or expanded. These policy areas included ethnic minority employment; health and social care for older people; homeless hostel provision; correctional services and the National Offender Management Service; and children and young people's services. The Review also looked more widely at the role of TSOs in public services, including the role of local partnerships and co-ordination between government funders.

**2.3** These initiatives to strengthen the sector's capacity need to be complemented by steps to improve departments' and other funders' capacity to work with the sector to achieve value for money. In the rest of this Part, we examine the progress being made by departments.

## Most departments have introduced some initiatives to improve their staff's skills

**2.4** Within central departments, there may be many separate units involved in funding of the sector, awarding grants and agreeing contracts for a wide range of purposes. At the Home Office, for example, at least 13 different units fund some third sector work, from crime prevention and drug counselling services to long-term funding for the charity for victims of crime, Victim Support.

**2.5** Ahead of the production and implementation of departmental strategies, departments' Grade 3 Champions and Voluntary and Community Sector Liaison Officers have begun to use various tools and processes to develop their funders' skills in dealing with the sector. There is no standard approach **(Figure 7)**.

**2.6** Most departments as yet have only a fragmented approach to developing their staff's capacity to work with the sector. Only half of the departments we examined have specific targets for developing their relationships with the sector. Corporate targets may include the sector indirectly or by implication; for example, the Department of Health has a general target to increase choice in health services.

**2.7** Most departments, however, have in place or are developing proposals for guidance and other mechanisms for developing funders' capacity. Several departments told us that they were still in the process of drafting guidance or developing policy. Others, more than two years after the Treasury Review was published, are still only at the stage of 'hoping' to take action. Some departments have a wide range of initiatives to improve their capacity; the Home Office and the Department for International Development are notable examples here. However, in general it was often unclear from departments' responses whether such initiatives have been widely adopted across departments' funding programmes. The quality and consistency of implementation may thus be variable.

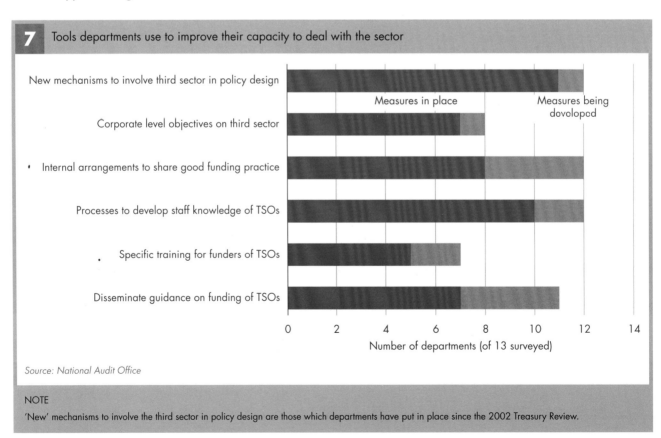

**7** Tools departments use to improve their capacity to deal with the sector

New mechanisms to involve third sector in policy design

Corporate level objectives on third sector

• Internal arrangements to share good funding practice

Processes to develop staff knowledge of TSOs

• Specific training for funders of TSOs

Disseminate guidance on funding of TSOs

Measures in place · Measures being developed

Number of departments (of 13 surveyed)

*Source: National Audit Office*

NOTE

'New' mechanisms to involve the third sector in policy design are those which departments have put in place since the 2002 Treasury Review.

## There are few specific training programmes

**2.8** There is relatively little evidence that departments are going beyond providing guidance, to actively train their staff in good funding practices. Only five of the 13 departments surveyed had established specific training programmes (see Figure 7). Comprehensive training appears to be easier to implement where the department concerned works with the sector in one specific area of service delivery. Where departments' funding streams are many and various, training is likely to be more ad-hoc or on-the-job, and considered the responsibility of the unit concerned rather than the department as a whole. However, two departments with relatively complex funding relationships – the Office of the Deputy Prime Minister and the Department for Environment, Food and Rural Affairs – said they were planning to introduce training programmes for their own staff involved in funding.

**2.9** Some departments have employed staff from the third sector. For example, the Department for Transport seconded a Community Liaison Manager from the third sector to implement the department's voluntary and community sector strategy.

**2.10** Those departments that have worked to develop their staff's ability to engage with the sector find that their efforts are appreciated. TSOs we consulted particularly praised initiatives by the Department for International Development (**see Case example 1**), the Home Office, the Department for Work and Pensions and the Department for Education and Skills, though they pointed out that increased willingness to engage with the sector did not necessarily mean that all aspects of poor funding practice had been addressed.

## Good intentions can be lost as funding flows through the delivery chain

**2.11** TSOs commonly draw on funding from a wide variety of public bodies, depending on the nature of their activities, their location and their awareness of what is available. For example, a local TSO we consulted received funding from several central government departments and other bodies, including core funding and contracts for service delivery, as well as funding from its local Primary Care Trusts and money from fundraising.

---

### CASE EXAMPLE 1

**Training and networking at the Department for International Development**

The Department for International Development works with a wide variety of TSOs who help its work to reduce poverty in developing countries. Its partners include UK-based major charities such as Oxfam and Christian Aid, and a range of local TSOs based in developing countries.

The department provides guidance on funding TSOs as part of its general induction training for all staff. A more detailed staff guide and on-the-job training is available for staff whose roles focus on TSO funding.

The department also has a range of initiatives which are designed to promote better linkages with the sector and encourage staff to share good practice, including an intranet site and a virtual network. It provides funding for BOND, a network of voluntary organisations working in international development, and holds regular meetings with other international development donors such as the European Commission and Comic Relief, to share good practice.

**2.12** Increasing amounts of government funding to the sector are channelled through other intermediary 'tiers' of government, such as executive agencies, NDPBs (non-departmental public bodies) and Regional Development Agencies. Health service contracts are managed at a local level by Primary Care Trusts and hospital trusts. Government Offices, part of central government based in the regions and working with local partners, are well placed to take decisions on funding to TSOs. **Figure 8 overleaf** shows the range of funding bodies.

**2.13** Good funding practices adopted by central government departments are generally not preserved where there are complex chains of intermediaries, passing funding from central government through non-departmental public bodies and executive agencies, layers of regional and local administration to local TSOs (**Figure 9 overleaf**). Decisions on funding practice will rest with managers outside central government departments, who are at least one remove from the civil servant networks responsible for implementing the Treasury Review's recommendations. Changes to funding processes have generally only been made if they are in line with the organisation's wider objectives and strategy. Indeed, the National Audit Office believes that the complexities and and transaction costs of filtering money through a variety of organisations until it reaches the front line should be simplified and reduced wherever possible.

**8**     Funding flows from government bodies to the third sector

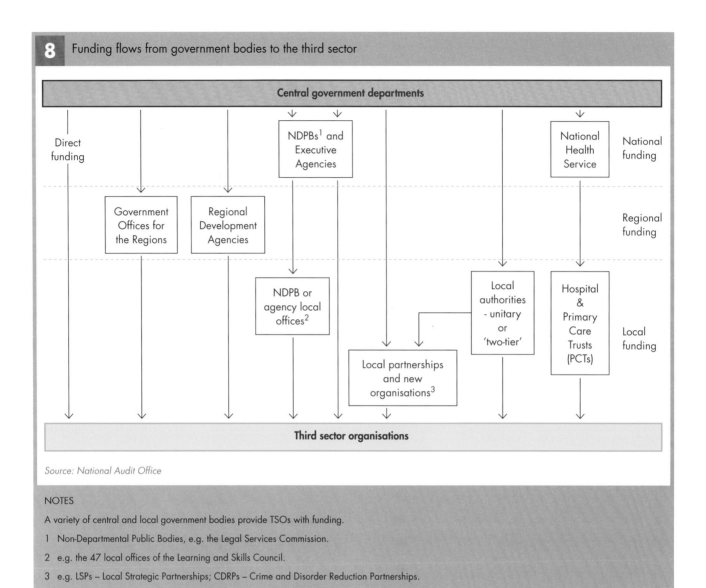

Source: National Audit Office

NOTES

A variety of central and local government bodies provide TSOs with funding.

1  Non-Departmental Public Bodies, e.g. the Legal Services Commission.

2  e.g. the 47 local offices of the Learning and Skills Council.

3  e.g. LSPs – Local Strategic Partnerships; CDRPs – Crime and Disorder Reduction Partnerships.

**9**     Dilution of good funding practice: examples from the National Audit Office research

■ A large national TSO, partly funded by the Supporting People scheme, reported that funding practices by the local authorities administering it were inconsistent[30] and not aligned with the Treasury Review recommendations. Full cost recovery was particularly problematic.

*"There's a fundamental failure to understand, a major education and training job".*

Source: National Audit Office

**2.14** There has been only limited effort by central government departments to disseminate good funding practices to their associated 'tiers of government'; six departments have issued written guidance. Other mechanisms for spreading good practice, such as seminars, working groups and web guidance, have been used by only one or two departments. Some departments, such as the Department for Transport and the Department of Trade and Industry, expect to publish such guidance during 2005. The Department of Health is currently working with TSOs and National Health Service (NHS) representatives to develop improvements in the procurement of health services from the third sector.

30     The Summary of this report notes the need for further research into local funding practices.

**2.15** The Government Offices for the Regions work as part of central government, to deliver central departments' public service targets. The Government Offices have worked with Home Office officials, and have set up several joint initiatives aimed at improving funding relationships between government and TSOs **(see Case example 2)**.

**2.16** Local government is a major source of TSO funding. Although there is very little reliable data available, the Home Office estimates that for the financial year 2001-02, (the latest year for which figures are available), local authorities distributed £1.87 billion to TSOs in England, around 29 per cent of the total £6.37 billion in TSO funding (including funding for housing associations). Many local authorities have drawn up Local Compacts with the sector, which in theory should improve funding practices. However, TSOs we consulted said that even where Local Compacts existed, the funding practices they recommend were often not adhered to. Pressure on local authority budgets meant that lowering the price of a service was often seen as more important than good funding practices such as full cost recovery.

---

## CASE EXAMPLE 2

### Sector funding initiatives by the Government Offices for the Regions (GOs)

The Government Office for the East Midlands (GOEM) has piloted a training course for staff involved with TSO funding, developed in collaboration with a local sector representative organisation. It hopes to make the course available to other government departments and agencies. GOEM has mapped sector funding across its region and is developing a panel of funding managers who will examine how funding is prioritised. GOEM has also set up a regional Compact website.

Three Government Offices for the Regions (GO Yorkshire and Humberside, GO South West and GO London) are responsible for regional 'lead funder' pilot schemes to streamline access and monitoring arrangements for TSOs seeking funding from multiple government sources. Further details of the 'lead funder' approach are given in Part 4 of this report.

---

**2.17** Local government representatives we consulted agreed that there was pressure on local authority budgets. However, they also reported that very few local authorities were aware of the Treasury Review recommendations or the thinking behind them, such as the need to build capacity in the sector. Where local authorities were aware, central government had given them no incentive to act on the recommendations.[31] Where changes had taken place – for example, streamlined procurement processes implemented by some local authorities – these were part of trends which had developed over the last five years or more, were not specific to authorities' use of the voluntary sector and were unrelated to the Treasury Review. In February 2005, the Treasury announced further steps to improve the partnership between local government and the sector.

**2.18** A new mechanism for improving co-ordination between central government, local authorities and other bodies including third sector organisations has been pilot-tested in 21 local authority areas since March 2004. These "Local Area Agreements" bring together the funding streams from central government going into an area, aiming to join up public services more effectively and allow greater flexibility for local solutions. Guidance on Local Area Agreements, issued by the Office of the Deputy Prime Minister, emphasises the importance of involving TSOs and has been welcomed by them.

## The sector has not yet seen the impact of the changes that have been made

**2.19** TSOs told us that government funders still had a long way to go in working effectively with the sector. They acknowledged the government's declared commitment to increasing the sector's involvement in public services. However, this high-level commitment had not noticeably influenced funders' approaches, they said, although there were exceptions **(see Case example 3)**. They had seen little practical change since the Treasury Review in 2002. In some cases TSOs themselves had to inform funders of new funding guidelines, such as those published by the Treasury.

---

31    In the course of our research, however, we found that the Office of the Deputy Prime Minister and other bodies which influence local authorities, including the Local Government Association and the improvement and development agency IDeA, have recognised the importance of TSOs as partners for local authorities and have incorporated this into their work.

**2.20** TSOs told us that many government funders did not properly understand their organisations or appreciate them as professional service-providers. This was sometimes the result of rapid turnover of staff in departments. The TSOs felt that government funders were often over-concerned with measurable outputs rather than less tangible, but sometimes more significant, outcomes for the users concerned. A focus on costs, beyond the level of scrutiny that would be applied to a private sector supplier, was widespread. Successful funding relationships often depended on the individual funding manager involved, rather than on corporate processes or guidelines, but this could leave successful relationships vulnerable to the effects of staff changes.

**2.21** Our research findings are in accordance with those of other organisations. For example, the Association of Chief Executives of Voluntary Organisations (ACEVO) carried out a survey of 74 chief executives of voluntary organisations in February 2005, in which 53 respondents (72 per cent) said that their funders' overall policy or practice had either stayed the same or had got worse in the past three years. Only 21 (28 per cent) had seen improvements.

## CASE EXAMPLE 3

### London Development Agency

TSOs we consulted valued the London Development Agency highly as a funder. The Agency's primary objective is the economic development of London and it works with both private and third sector organisations to achieve this. TSOs particularly praised the Agency's voluntary sector department. Staff were very accessible, supportive and helpful to TSOs, despite their sometimes complicated tender processes, they said.

*"I've noticed a positive change in, for example, the LDA in London…they've got officials who are particularly up to date with what's happening in central London, vis à vis full cost recovery, so they're reminding people like me to 'Make sure you bid for full cost recovery'."*

The Agency is currently developing a new strategy for its relationship with the sector, which will focus on improving the balance of risk between itself and the TSOs it funds.

It should be noted, however, that the London Development Agency was an exception to TSOs' general opinion of Regional Development Agencies as funders. TSOs generally felt that the Regional Development Agencies' primary objectives were economic rather than social, which led them to focus on the needs of business rather than the third sector. However, the Department of Trade and Industry, the central government department with lead responsibility for the nine Regional Development Agencies, said that six of them were in the process of reviewing their regional economic strategies in line with new guidance which gave more focus to the third sector.

# PART THREE
## Funding methods are highly variable across government

**3.1** The choice of funding method is crucial to the achievement of value for money. Before any work is done, officials must decide on the form that funding is to take: whether to use a grant or a contract, and what the terms of the agreement will be, such as the period of funding, the timing of payments and which of the providers' costs they are prepared to meet.

**3.2** A poor funding method could place unacceptable risks on the TSO, or involve a disproportionate cost of administration in relation to the sums involved. At the other extreme, a poor funding mechanism might provide insufficient protection for the funding department. A poor funding arrangement could also distort choices between public, private or third sector providers. Any of these outcomes is likely to result in poor value for money.

**3.3** Government has provided departments with guidance on appropriate funding methods in a range of circumstances. The Treasury has produced and widely disseminated its 'Guidance to Funders'. The existing Compact code of good funding practice, originally published in 2000, was updated and reissued in March 2005. In addition, the Home Office has issued procurement guidance.[32] This Part examines how far departments and their associated public bodies have improved their funding methods.

# The form of funding needs to be tailored to objectives

**3.4** In the sections that follow, we demonstrate that funding for the sector is beset by inconsistent practice and confusion over when to use different funding methods. One reason for this is that funding to the sector covers a wide range of purposes and circumstances, to which funding methods need to be tailored. Funders need to be clear about their aims before determining the most appropriate method; a useful starting point is to consider whether they are engaged in supporting a worthy cause ('giving'), procuring services ('shopping') or in building capacity in the sector ('investing').[33] Greater clarity about the purpose of funding would also help reduce TSOs' uncertainties about the basis on which they will be funded.

**3.5** Each type of relationship between funder and recipient has distinct characteristics:

- A 'giving' approach might be more appropriate where the funder wishes to provide general support or a contribution, but does not define the expected outputs, allowing the recipient to decide on the best use of the funds;

- A funder 'shopping' for a supplier – for example to provide residential care services for the elderly – will be concerned with the cost and quality of the service, and might decide to use a competitive tendering process involving a range of private and third sector suppliers;

32 See footnote 26 on page 16 of this report.
33 Concept taken from 'The Grantmaking Tango: Issues for Funders' by Julia Unwin, Baring Foundation 2004.

■ An 'investing' funder will be seeking a long-term outcome from the spending, such as policy change or developments in the organisation's or sector's capacity.

**3.6** The 'shopping' approach is closest to "public service delivery" and is more likely to require a tightly-specified contract and procurement process, in which the sector may compete with in-house or private sector providers. In contrast, 'investing' and 'giving' are more likely to require conventional grant-making approaches.

**3.7** It is important to note here that while some government departments thought the concepts of 'giving', 'shopping' and 'investing' were useful distinctions, others felt that the concepts were not easy to apply in practice and would require further elaboration.

## There is little settled practice on whether to use grants, contracts or procurement

### Government funders are inconsistent in their funding approaches

**3.8** Most departments say that they make use of both 'grants' and 'contracts' in funding the sector, although there is no common understanding of the scope of the two terms. Funders frequently refer to the two types of funding arrangement as follows:

■ Grants – tend to be smaller payments, for a purpose which may be defined in detail or in broad terms, based on trust with little scope for the recipient to appeal if the grant is cancelled. They are likely to be appropriate for situations where the purpose of funding is 'giving' or 'investing';

■ Contracts[34] – larger payments, for purposes defined by the funders, linked to tightly-defined objectives and establishing a legal relationship between funder and recipient. Contracts are also likely to be associated with formal procurement methods and rules.

**3.9** Only five of the 13 departments we surveyed had any established policy or guidance to help funders design the most appropriate funding mechanism. Where guidance existed, it had been produced relatively recently, in 2003 or 2004. Some other departments were developing policies on this issue at the time of our research. There is as yet no central or definitive source to which funders can refer.

### Lack of consistent funding practice causes difficulty for TSOs

**3.10** TSOs we consulted reported a variety of problems related to this confusion over the distinction between 'grants' and 'contracts' and when it was most appropriate to use each method. There was an increasing tendency by funders to favour contract-type funding arrangements, often involving competitive tendering, over grants.

**3.11** Other TSOs, particularly larger organisations with established management processes, did not object to the increasing emphasis on contracts. However, they also reported that funders applied contracts in ways which ran counter to value for money. These TSOs believed that funders ran contracting processes which involved TSOs differently from contracting situations including only private sector suppliers. In general, contracting processes involving TSOs allowed little scope for negotiation over contract terms and sought excessive amounts of information in bids for funding. Funders often sought to 'claw back'[35] any surplus funds remaining at the end of the contract from TSOs, while private sector suppliers would retain these as their profit. The types of contract available to TSOs were generally much less diverse than for the private sector; processes such as strategic partnerships and framework agreements were much less widely used in third sector funding.

**3.12** It should be noted, too, that poorly conceived and managed funding schemes, with inappropriate mixing of procurement and grant arrangements, could also be disadvantageous to potential private sector providers of services. For best value for money, neither third sector nor private providers should be disadvantaged.

---

34 In law, a contract requires an offer and a corresponding acceptance; a consideration (meaning an exchange of payment or something else of value); and an intention to create legal relations.

35 In February 2005, the Treasury announced new rules to reduce the extent of claw-back provisions in relation to assets acquired with grant funding, to bring these more into line with the way the private sector is treated when working with government. But the issue of TSO surplus and its claw-back remains.

**3.13** TSOs also highlighted a general lack of clarity over the legal distinction between grants and contracts. Grant arrangements often had the same four key elements as contracts: an offer, an acceptance of the offer, a consideration (e.g. payment), and the intention to create legal relations. Where this was the case, payments should be subject to funders' procurement processes, European Union procurement rules and European Union rules on state aid, if these apply to the size of payment concerned.[36]

## Grant-in-aid is a special form of funding which may be appropriate in some circumstances

**3.14** Grant-in-aid, a funding mechanism with a more relaxed level of control, is normally used for departments' funding of their non-departmental public bodies (NDPBs), rather than in funding the sector. In practice, though, some well-established voluntary or charitable organisations which are not NDPBs (such as the National Council for Voluntary Organisations) receive grant-in-aid. These arrangements allow greater certainty about continuity of funding, but leave the recipient greater discretion to allocate funds and design programmes, subject to strategic discussion with

the funder. As more TSOs establish longer-term strategic funding relationships with government, the grant-in-aid model may become more widespread.

## Full cost recovery continues to be a major problem

**3.15** A key issue highlighted by the Treasury Review was the failure of funders and providers to allow for 'full cost recovery'. Full cost recovery means that TSOs receive payment not only for the direct costs they incur by providing a service – for example, staff salaries in the case of residential care services – but also for overhead costs such as the costs of office space, utilities and information technology services, as well as various other costs such as depreciation[37] and interest on loans. **Figure 10** provides further details. Failure to recover full costs can mean that TSOs have to divert funding intended for service provision into paying overheads, or subsidise service provision from other sources such as donor income. Ultimately, failure to cover overheads may lead to organisations shrinking or collapsing.

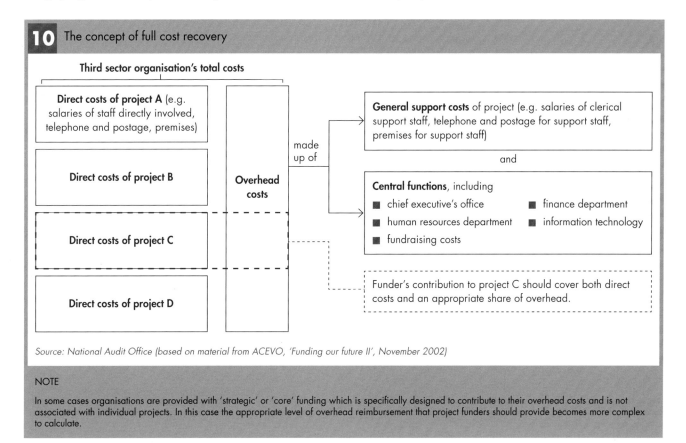

**10** The concept of full cost recovery

**Third sector organisation's total costs**

**Direct costs of project A** (e.g. salaries of staff directly involved, telephone and postage, premises)

**Direct costs of project B**

**Direct costs of project C**

**Direct costs of project D**

**Overhead costs**

made up of

**General support costs** of project (e.g. salaries of clerical support staff, telephone and postage for support staff, premises for support staff)

and

**Central functions**, including
- chief executive's office
- human resources department
- fundraising costs
- finance department
- information technology

Funder's contribution to project C should cover both direct costs and an appropriate share of overhead.

Source: National Audit Office (based on material from ACEVO, 'Funding our future II', November 2002)

NOTE

In some cases organisations are provided with 'strategic' or 'core' funding which is specifically designed to contribute to their overhead costs and is not associated with individual projects. In this case the appropriate level of overhead reimbursement that project funders should provide becomes more complex to calculate.

36  Some departments felt that service level agreements, which are not subject to procurement processes, were a useful mechanism for clarifying funding arrangements.
37  A cost used in organisations' accounts to allow for the declining value of long-term assets such as buildings.

**3.16** Just as private organisations cover their overhead costs from revenue raised, TSOs need to fund their overheads from their income. But in the past, TSOs had too often bid on the basis of direct costs alone, or were unaware of the full cost of their activities, and funders had been reluctant to meet all the costs of providing a service. The Treasury 2002 Review acknowledged the problem and recommended that "All departments… (should ensure) that the price for contracts reflects the full cost of the service, including the legitimate portion of overhead costs".[38]

## 'Full cost recovery' is inseparable from the choice of funding approach

**3.17** Full cost recovery is linked to the choice of funding method (grant or contract), as shown in **Figure 11** below, because of the importance of overhead costs to the negotiation of a contract or the award of a grant:

■ Ideally, a TSO (or a private company) bidding for a contract should submit a price based on a clear understanding of the overhead costs that the organisation needs to cover, as well as the direct costs associated with delivering the contract. In general, however, the details of overhead costs would not be disclosed to the funder, nor should the funder seek this information since it would not normally be expected from a private sector supplier.

■ In the case of grants, the application of full cost recovery will depend on the purpose of the grant: 'giving' or 'investing' as described in the section above. Costing, rather than pricing, is likely to be the more appropriate basis for funding decisions. In some cases it will be appropriate for the funder to make a contribution to costs whilst in others they might be expected to cover full costs.

## Government funders have made limited progress on full cost recovery

**3.18** Our research shows that government departments have made some progress on allowing full cost recovery since the Treasury Review, but as yet this is very limited. Departments were generally aware of the principle of full cost recovery and supported it, although one questioned whether it is always and everywhere appropriate, and another commented that there is as yet no consensus on what 'full cost recovery' means, how it should be calculated and what should be paid for. Even within a single department, approaches to full cost recovery sometimes varied between funding divisions. TSOs generally considered that there had been a positive "change in government rhetoric" on full cost recovery, but felt that this had not been translated into practice nor adopted throughout all funding streams.

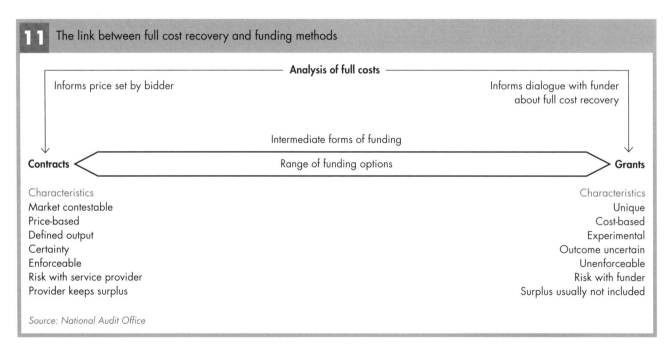

**11** The link between full cost recovery and funding methods

Analysis of full costs

Informs price set by bidder

Informs dialogue with funder about full cost recovery

Intermediate forms of funding

**Contracts**      Range of funding options      **Grants**

| Characteristics | Characteristics |
| --- | --- |
| Market contestable | Unique |
| Price-based | Cost-based |
| Defined output | Experimental |
| Certainty | Outcome uncertain |
| Enforceable | Unenforceable |
| Risk with service provider | Risk with funder |
| Provider keeps surplus | Surplus usually not included |

*Source: National Audit Office*

---

38     *'The role of the voluntary and community sector in service delivery'* HM Treasury 2002, Recommendation 13.

**3.19** Of the 13 departments[39] included in our survey, eight were prepared to pay at least some overhead costs. Their approaches were variable, however, including:

- requirements for providers to specify and account for overhead costs in detail;

- adding a small proportion of direct funding to be used for overheads (at the Department for International Development, 8-10 per cent of project funding can be used for overheads), rather than assessing actual overheads; and

- undefined terms such as a "financial contribution" towards overheads, or "a legitimate proportion" of overheads.

Those departments who did not clearly state that they were prepared to pay overhead costs, either had reservations about whether full cost recovery was appropriate in all circumstances or preferred to adopt 'formula funding' approaches (e.g. paying a flat rate per customer served) and left applicants to judge whether the rate set would cover their full costs.

**3.20** TSOs told us that despite the Treasury Review's recommendations it was common for funders to refuse to cover certain types of overhead. Funders would usually ask TSOs to reveal their overhead costs in detail and would then decide which costs they were prepared to cover. TSOs believed that private sector firms bidding for contracts would usually submit only a price and would not be required to provide details of their overheads.

**3.21** Departments and the sector identified a number of stumbling-blocks which prevent the principle of full cost recovery being applied effectively:

- **lack of cost information** – TSOs, particularly small organisations, often could not evaluate their overhead costs effectively and allocate them to their various projects, because they lacked financial expertise, staff or management information. Following the Treasury Review, the Association of Chief Executives of Voluntary Organisations (ACEVO) has produced guidance for the sector on how to identify their costs and assign them to projects. The guidance has since been simplified and updated;[40]

- **lack of agreement on which costs should be funded** – funders and TSOs both felt unclear on what costs should be included – for example, whether a proportion of the TSO's costs for its general public relations and marketing activities should be paid for by government funders, or whether a proportion of central management costs should be included in a local office's contracts;

- **lack of clear and practical guidance** – although there is useful guidance on full cost recovery from ACEVO and the Treasury, funders and TSOs felt it should be supplemented to include more practical worked examples;

- **inconsistency in practice at a local level** – our evidence suggests that local authority funders are even less likely than central government to allow full cost recovery. TSOs told us that local authorities generally either were not aware of the Treasury recommendation or "ignored" it; authorities were often focused on cost control to keep within their budgets;

- **'strings attached'** – some funders require TSOs to provide 'match funding' when awarding a contract or grant, and that the TSO contribution should cover management and other overhead charges.

**3.22** Guidance issued by ACEVO has helped TSOs understand their costs, to inform pricing or costing decisions and bids for funds. However, itemisation of (and subsequent accounting for) overhead costs in detail is unlikely to be appropriate in a procurement process and may be less than helpful in a grant-making situation: funding bids may be constructed when the TSO cannot be sure about the number of bids that will succeed, or the scale of their activity; as a result, overheads may not work out exactly as predicted, for good reasons. In these circumstances, a mark-up based on a realistic view of overhead rates would avoid an over-emphasis on the itemisation of overhead costs both large and small.

39    In some cases, a department's relationship with the third sector occurs primarily via its 'sponsored bodies'(NDPBs and/or executive agencies), and the response to the questionnaire will have been made by the relevant sponsored body, e.g. the Legal Services Commission in the case of the Department for Constitutional Affairs.
40    'Full Cost Recovery: a guide and toolkit on cost-allocation' ACEVO and New Philanthropy Capital 2004.

**3.23** Overall, full cost recovery appears to be one of the most difficult issues for funders and the sector to resolve. Examples of poor practice or alleged poor practice were far more widespread in our research than examples of success – in part, we suspect, because of the failure to specify the purpose of funding and understand how full cost recovery should be applied. One major TSO's account of its difficulties securing full cost recovery is given in **Case example 4**.

## Payment in advance is now relatively common

**3.24** 'End loading' of payments, where TSOs receive payment only after the agreed work has been completed, can cause serious cash-flow problems for TSOs with limited funds or working capital. End-loading deters some TSOs from even applying for funding, if they will not be able to bear the running costs in the meantime **(see Figure 12)**.

### There are now guidelines for making payments in advance of expenditure

**3.25** The Treasury Review recognised that end-loading of payments was "...perceived to be a major problem and a significant deterrent to working in partnership with government."[41] The Review acknowledged that the problem was partly due to varying interpretations of Government Accounting rules, whereby some departments believed that they were not permitted to make payments in advance of TSOs' expenditure. The Treasury promised to issue clear guidance to funders distinguishing payment in advance of expenditure, which is permitted, from payment in advance of need, which is not permitted. In September 2003, the Treasury published its promised guidance[42] and disseminated it to government departments, through a series of seminars during 2004. Most funders we contacted were familiar with the guidance.

---

### CASE EXAMPLE 4

**Turning Point's experiences of funders' approach to full cost recovery**

Turning Point is a national charity with an annual turnover of £55 million, which provides services for people with complex needs, including those affected by drug and alcohol misuse, mental health problems and those with a learning disability across England and Wales. Turning Point runs services from over 200 locations, employs nearly 2,000 people and is the largest provider of substance abuse services in the country. Its main funders are the National Health Service, local authority Social Services and Drug Action Teams (local co-ordinating groups set up under the government's national drugs strategy).

Chief executive Lord Victor Adebowale said securing full cost recovery was very rare and had occurred only where Turning Point had improved its ability to negotiate contracts. Ultimately, Turning Point was prepared to close services down if funding was not sustainable.

*"The deal is it's either sustainable or it goes, because if it's not sustainable, sooner or later the quality drops and our name's above the door. We've got to protect those clients at the end of the day. If we don't achieve full cost recovery...then those clients are getting a poor service."*

*Source: National Audit Office*

---

**12** Advance payment: example from the National Audit Office research

A group representing local TSOs in east London told us that local groups had in the past been unable to arrange advance payment from the local authority since the authority had not signed up to a local Compact and therefore did not practice good funding principles. Advance funding was vital to the proposed work, which would be carried out by small specialist groups targeting black and minority ethnic people:

*"These are the sorts of circumstances for groups which have no paid workers, a budget which is probably in single figure thousands if they're lucky, who are now being asked to spend their money and then get it back."*

However, recently the local authority had changed its approach, in part due to guidance from the Treasury and the Home Office, the group added. Requests for advance payments were now being responded to, and the authority was working to develop a local Compact.

*Source: National Audit Office*

---

41      *'The role of the voluntary and community sector in service delivery: a cross cutting review'*, HM Treasury 2002, paragraph 6.7, page 26.
42      *'Guidance to Funders: Improving funding relationships for voluntary and community organisations,'* HM Treasury, September 2003.

## Central government funders often allow advance payments, but issues remain

**3.26** Most central government funders allow payment in advance, in at least some of their projects and programmes, in line with Treasury guidance to consider value for money rather than adopting advance payment wholesale. Ten of the 13 central government departments we surveyed could produce examples of payment in advance. In most cases departments had allowed payment in advance for some years, rather than introducing changes in response to the Treasury Review. The Legal Services Commission, the Department for Environment, Food and Rural Affairs (and the Countryside Agency), the Department for Culture, Media and Sport, the Department for International Development, the Department for Transport, the Office of the Deputy Prime Minister, the Home Office, the Department for Work and Pensions and the Department for Trade and Industry's Phoenix Fund all fell into this category.

**3.27** Treasury guidance says that a blanket approach to advance payment is "obviously inappropriate" and tells funders to "…consider applications for advance payments on a case-by-case basis".[43] Approaches to advance payment are consequently variable:

- some funders **limit advance payments to certain kinds of funding** such as capital, 'core' or 'strategic' funding;

- some **allow payment in advance if TSOs request it,** but would not automatically make advance payments;

- some allow payment in advance **for smaller sums,** but not for large contracts.

**3.28** These various approaches carry risks, for example: limiting advance payments to core or strategic funding does not allow advance funding for other large costs, such as the salaries of project staff. Awaiting requests for advance payment (rather than offering it) tests TSOs' negotiation skills rather than their ability to deliver; while restricting advance payment to smaller sums excludes smaller TSOs from bidding for large contracts.

**3.29** More appropriately, departments and other funders are adapting payment in advance to the circumstances of each grant or contract:

- **Timing** of payment varies, from paying a fixed proportion of the cost of a project 'up front', to annual, quarterly or monthly advance payments through the life of a project. One department, the Department of Trade and Industry, offered a variety of payment mechanisms which could be selected to suit the circumstances of the project;

- **Later payments are conditional on performance,** only being paid out if successful results are reported from the early stages of a project **(see Case example 5)**. Jobcentre Plus's Workstep and Innovation Fund programmes, both designed to help particular groups of people into work, use this approach with their TSO service-providers. In some cases, progress reports were required as frequently as every quarter.

**3.30** There are also connections between advance payment and other funding choices:

- advance payment, if offered as part of a contract or procurement, must also be available to private sector competitors; and

- advance payment is unlikely to be appropriate if financing costs are allowed to be included as part of full cost recovery.

---

### CASE EXAMPLE 5

**The Pension Service Partnership Fund**

The Pension Service Partnership Fund, which made its first funding awards to TSOs in 2004, funds in advance on an annual basis (it is a two year fund) with the second year's payment being dependent upon successful results from the first year. It makes payments of between £500 and £50,000 to organisations which help pensioners to take up benefits and allowances to which they are entitled, promote the independence of older people and improve access to services. All applications for funding must be endorsed by a local partner funder.

Recipients include Ace of Clubs, a day centre in Clapham, south London, which will use its Fund money to improve its benefits advice and welfare services. Ace of Clubs also operates a healthy eating project for elderly people, befriending and entertainment schemes and services for elderly homeless people and those with mental health problems.

The Pension Service Partnership Fund was launched in 2004, administered and largely funded by the Department for Work and Pensions, with a contribution from the Department for Environment, Food and Rural Affairs targeted at specific areas of rural poverty.

---

43   *Guidance to Funders: improving funding relationships for voluntary and community organisations',* HM Treasury 2003, page 14, paragraph 2.16.

## Payment in advance of expenditure is appreciated by the sector

**3.31** TSOs we consulted acknowledged that many government funders allowed advance payments, and welcomed this. Advance payments allowed TSOs a greater degree of independence, security and flexibility. The majority of TSOs who responded to the online consultation NCVO carried out had received at least some payment in advance **(Figure 13)**. However, TSOs did not report any noticeable change in funding practices since the Treasury Review in 2002. Their funders who allowed payment in advance had done so for some time and had not changed their practices in response to the Review or Treasury's subsequent guidance, as far as the TSOs were aware.

**3.32** Local authorities' attitudes to advance payment varied widely. Some TSOs reported advance payments being available, but more complained of payments made in arrears, late payments and even active resistance to the Treasury guidelines. They pointed out that commitment to the principle of paying in advance could only be regarded as hypothetical when payments arrived late, and therefore effectively in arrears.

## There are still challenges to be overcome

**3.33** Despite the widespread progress with advance payment, there is still confusion amongst some funders on the appropriate circumstances for advance payment. Participants in our research raised concerns that advance payments to the sector could break Government Accounting rules, either by:

■ incurring extra costs for the taxpayer, as interest on public funds was lost to the Exchequer; or

■ contravening European Union rules that all potential suppliers must be able to compete on equal terms.

Both these concerns are addressed in the Treasury's guidance to funders published in 2003 and in the Government Accounting manual itself[44], which was revised in March 2004 to exempt TSOs from the general principle that advance payments should be exceptional. However, our research shows that there is work to be done in raising awareness of these changes.

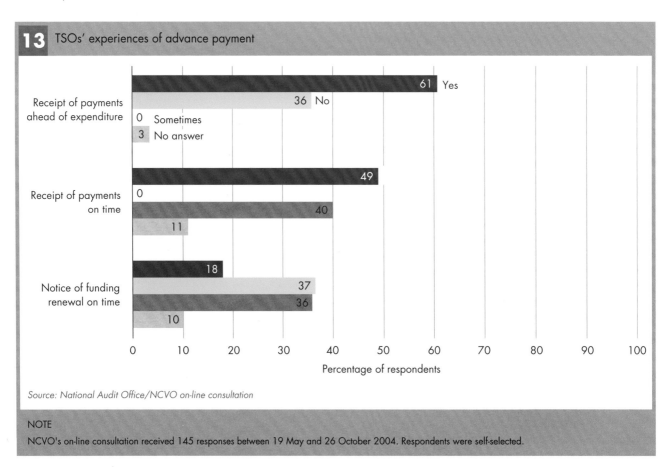

**13** TSOs' experiences of advance payment

Receipt of payments ahead of expenditure
- 61 Yes
- 36 No
- 0 Sometimes
- 3 No answer

Receipt of payments on time
- 49
- 0
- 40
- 11

Notice of funding renewal on time
- 18
- 37
- 36
- 10

Percentage of respondents

*Source: National Audit Office/NCVO on-line consultation*

NOTE

NCVO's on-line consultation received 145 responses between 19 May and 26 October 2004. Respondents were self-selected.

44    Government Accounting Annex 16.1, paragraph 2b.

**3.34** A few funders also mentioned practical problems with the administration of advance payments, including difficulties keeping track of spend against outcomes, and technological difficulties in some cases – for example, Jobcentre Plus IT systems do not currently support advance payments.

## There is little progress on longer-term funding

**3.35** TSOs depend on a variety of funding including legacies, donations and fundraising, and government funding. If much of this government funding has a limited life – one year or less – organisations can face a variety of problems, including:

- excessive time and resources spent on making funding applications;

- difficulty recruiting and retaining staff;

- short-term, unsustainable achievements which cease when the funding runs out; and

- limitations to TSOs' growth and development of new services.

**3.36** The 2002 Treasury Review acknowledged these difficulties and described the use of renewable one-year contracts as the principal cause for concern. Treasury guidance to government funders, published in 2003 as a follow-up to the Review, lays out the rationale for longer-term funding, defined as "funding arrangements that last more than one year." It recommends that funding bodies should endeavour to agree longer-term funding arrangements, if these represent good value for money. The guidance also pointed out that longer-term funding could often represent better value for money for government, by allowing them to focus on longer-term results.

### Changes to government budgeting processes make long-term funding easier

**3.37** Changes in the way government departments receive their funding from the Treasury mean that departments now have greater flexibility to set up longer-term funding arrangements than in the past, where this is appropriate to the service funded. Most significantly, departments no longer bid for their own budgets annually. Since 1998 most departments have had firm three year budgets, based on the government's Spending Reviews which take place every two years.[45] In its guidance to funders, the Treasury said these changes meant that "…there is…no fiscal barrier that prevents funding bodies from agreeing longer-term funding arrangements with recipients of funds, if it fulfils the objectives of that funding body and represents good value for money". In general, however, three-year budgets do not apply to departments' associated NDPBs and executive agencies, although Treasury guidance encourages departments to cascade three-year budgets to their associated NDPBs and agencies.

**3.38** Half of departments could not provide data on the length of their funding arrangements with the sector. Only seven of the 13 departments we surveyed could estimate the amount of their third sector funding that was provided for one year or less, and/or how much was agreed for longer periods. The Office of the Deputy Prime Minister in particular, which has complex funding relationships with the sector – much of its funding being distributed at local level through a wide variety of different partnerships – said it would be "virtually impossible" to estimate the proportion of funding given according to timescale. Nevertheless ODPM does not believe that any of its programmes are formally restricted to less than a 3-year cycle unless they are specifically aimed at supporting 'one-off' projects. The Office of the Deputy Prime Minister also pointed out that it plans to introduce three-year grant settlements for local authorities from 2006-2007, which would allow local authorities to set up longer-term funding arrangements with TSOs.

**3.39** Based on the limited data, there are wide variations in the progress departments have made on this issue. While only 3 per cent (£2.5 million) of the Department for Transport's funding to the sector is provided for one year or less, at the Department for Environment, Food and Rural Affairs 24 per cent of sector funding was for one year or less, while for the Home Office, the figure was 72 per cent. Departments should not necessarily allocate all of their TSO funding to long-term arrangements, since particular policy areas may require a larger or smaller proportion of the total funding 'pot' to be provided under long-term arrangements, but there is no evidence that the proportions quoted for the three departments above are appropriate to their particular policy objectives.

**3.40** There is also relatively little information available about changes in the pattern of funding arrangements since 2002; again, only seven of the 13 departments we surveyed could provide any information. None quantified the extent of the change, but gave examples of particular funding streams which have moved to longer-term funding arrangements. Some of these are described in **Case example 6 to Case example 9 overleaf**.

---

45    The third year of the budget acts as a fixed baseline for the next Spending Review.

## CASE EXAMPLE 6

**Home Office long-term funding for crime reduction**

The Home Office's Crime Reduction Directorate, part of the Crime Reduction and Community Safety Group, has changed its national grant funding agreements from one to three-year rolling agreements. Grant recipients are given an indication of the next three years' funding levels and these are reviewed and updated annually in consultation with the funded organisation.

The Crime Reduction Directorate is responsible for £1.85 million in direct grant funding each year, including £1 million for a national domestic violence helpline and core funding for Crimestoppers and Crime Concern. The directorate also distributes funds to local Crime and Disorder Reduction Partnerships (CDRPs). Home Office decided to make the change in response to the Treasury Review's recommendations and a report by the NAO.[46] Following consultation, funded partners have welcomed the change.

## CASE EXAMPLE 7

**Strategic TSO funding at the Department for International Development (DfID)**

DfID has a series of long-term funding agreements with major TSOs involved in international development work, such as Oxfam, ActionAid and Save the Children. These agreements, known as Partnership Programme Agreements (PPAs), set out how the organisations will work with DfID to meet international development targets. The agreements currently last for three to five years and include a commitment to the amount of strategic funding that DfID will provide over the life of the agreement. They range from £3.6 million per year to more than £24 million per year. Many agreements provide between 7-12 per cent of the TSO's total funding. DfID is currently considering a proposal to extend all the PPAs to six years, in order to provide more funding stability. The PPAs are due to be re-negotiated during 2005.

The Department also has long-term Strategic Grant Agreements (SGAs), typically worth around £330,000 per year, with UK-based organisations who work with DfID to build support for international development. TSOs funded under these arrangements include Connections for Development, representing black and minority ethnic voluntary organisations and the regeneration charity Groundwork UK. The SGAs typically last for three years.

## CASE EXAMPLE 8

**Department for Work and Pensions (DWP)**

DWP has funded Better Government for Older People (BGOP) since 2001. The organisation, a partnership between several charities including Age Concern and Help the Aged, aims to ensure that older people help to influence government strategies and services for an ageing population. Initially, the small amount of funding available was due to last for one year, but since BGOP did not generate sufficient funding from other sources, DWP reviewed its provision and from 2002-03 began to provide more substantial core funding. BGOP now has grant-in-aid funding until March 2006.

## CASE EXAMPLE 9

**Special Grants Programme (Office of the Deputy Prime Minister)**

The Special Grants Programme run by the Office of the Deputy Prime Minister supports innovative work by TSOs in line with ODPM's objectives of community development and regeneration. In the financial year 2005-06 it will allocate a total of £2.25 million to around 20 organisations; grant sizes usually range from £10,000 to £80,000. One current recipient, the Association of British Credit Unions, has used Special Grants Programme funding to train some of its credit union members in financial monitoring processes which improve both their effectiveness and financial performance.

Special Grants Programme funding is granted for either five years, for 'strategic' funding of TSOs' normal programmes of work, or up to three years in the case of 'development funding' for specific projects. TSOs we spoke to welcomed the programme's scope to provide longer-term funding to continue their usual activities, rather than having to redesign their activities to meet funders' requirements.

## The sector has seen no significant change

**3.41** TSOs had not noticed any general trend towards government departments funding for the longer-term, despite a recognition by funders that longer-term funding was desirable **(Figure 14)**. They looked forward to future developments, but had not yet seen much evidence of action. Most felt that their funding relationship with government did not allow them to plan more than a year ahead with certainty **(see Figure 15)**.

46 'Reducing crime: the Home Office working with Crime and Disorder Reduction Partnerships', HC16 2004-05, 1 December 2004.

**14** Difficulties with long-term funding: example from the National Audit Office research

A large national TSO engaged in health service delivery compared the National Health Service's engagement with the sector unfavourably to its use of private sector suppliers:

*"The sector has...the asset base, we have the ability to raise money, we have the ability to borrow capital but we need 10-15 year contracts to make that even remotely viable. And yet, when (government funders) talk about this, they say 'Be grateful if you get a three-year contract' whereas under the Private Finance Initiative, 10, 20 year contracts are the norm."*

*Source: National Audit Office*

**3.42** Many organisations favoured funding for five years or longer, particularly where funding was being used either for major capital acquisitions or for long-term services, such as care for adults with learning difficulties. TSOs considered that long-term funding arrangements would improve the sector's professionalism and allow TSOs to raise money from the private sector.

## Funders still see risks in long-term funding

**3.43** Many funders still perceive barriers to setting up long-term arrangements. A key concern raised in our research was the risk of becoming 'locked-in' to certain suppliers, with two potentially damaging effects:

- if the quality of the service declined over time, funders feared they would not be able to address it by removing funding;

- longer-term funding could exclude new and innovative service-providers from consideration.

**3.44** Treasury guidance addresses the first concern, suggesting that funding arrangements should be structured to provide incentives to maintain standards over the long term, for example by providing an initial fixed sum and making subsequent payments subject to satisfactory delivery. The guidance lacks practical suggestions to address the risk of excluding new third sector providers.[47]

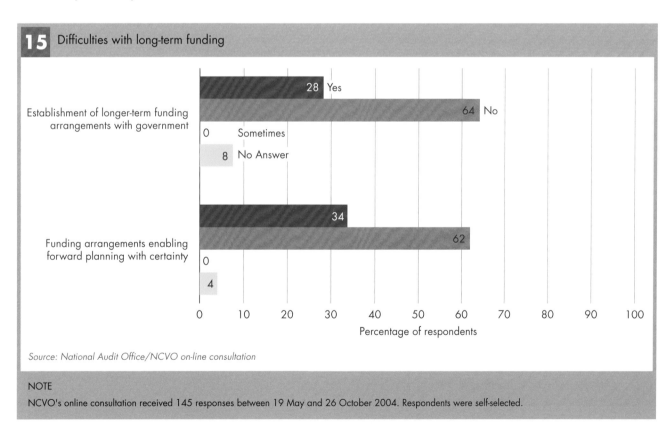

**15** Difficulties with long-term funding

Establishment of longer-term funding arrangements with government
- 28 Yes
- 64 No
- 0 Sometimes
- 8 No Answer

Funding arrangements enabling forward planning with certainty
- 34
- 62
- 0
- 4

Percentage of respondents

*Source: National Audit Office/NCVO on-line consultation*

NOTE
NCVO's online consultation received 145 responses between 19 May and 26 October 2004. Respondents were self-selected.

47    This point has a clear parallel in government procurement from the private sector, where long-term contracts may carry an equal risk of excluding new suppliers. The Office of Government Commerce has undertaken various work to encourage government departments to employ a diverse range of suppliers; there may be useful lessons here for TSO funding arrangements.

**3.45** Some funders identified other barriers which could prevent them from moving funding programmes to longer-term arrangements:

■   Budgeting processes within departments. Although departments' budgets are set for three years, programme and policy teams within departments may have their budgets agreed annually and therefore feel unable to commit funds for longer than one year. However, this concern could be addressed by providing provisional funding beyond one year, as described above.

■   The increased amount of staff resources required to negotiate long term strategic agreements. This concern appears to be unfounded; other funders who had put long-term arrangements in place said that administrative work was significantly reduced, since annual funding rounds were no longer necessary. However, long-term funding agreements may require a more detailed initial negotiation and greater involvement by senior staff.

# Late confirmation of funding is commonplace

**3.46** Where contracts are subject to regular renewal, timely notification of the renewal is important to allow TSOs to maintain the continuity of the service. One of the most frequent problems TSOs mentioned was their inability, without a confirmed contract renewal, to offer secure employment to project staff. By the time the contract was renewed, key staff could already have left to take up employment elsewhere.

**3.47** TSOs we consulted reported that it was common for their government funders to confirm funding agreements late, even some time after the agreed start of a time-critical project – only 18 per cent of funding renewals were on time (Figure 13 on page 34). In some cases, confirmation was late even where funders had recognised the need for advance payments to allow TSOs to cover the running costs of their work.

## PART FOUR
# There has been some progress on streamlining application and monitoring processes

**4.1** Once the fundamental aspects of a funding programme have been decided, government funders must also determine administrative aspects such as how to attract applicants and select recipients of funding and how the results of the work will be monitored. The Treasury Review recognised that appropriate funding administration is as important to successful funding relationships with the sector as the funding method (discussed in Part 3 of this report). This Part therefore discusses the extent to which government funders have improved their funding administration.

## Information and application processes have improved since 2002

**4.2** TSOs commonly depend on a variety of funding sources of varying sizes, timescales and purposes. A single TSO may make funding applications to several different central, regional or local government funders. These applications commonly require TSOs to submit a large amount of written information, covering not only the project for which the funding is to be used, but also a great deal of detailed information about the applicant organisation. When a TSO has several funders, the amount of management time spent on funding applications can quickly become excessive. Meanwhile, funders need to be able to identify the best providers and assure themselves that public money is being well-spent.

**4.3** The 2002 Treasury Review recommended that government funders should work together to streamline their application processes, primarily by developing a common point of access for central government grant aid and strategic funding.

## Government funders have made changes

**4.4** Since the Treasury Review, government funders have introduced a number of changes to funding information and application processes. There is as yet no comprehensive, 'one-stop shop' for information on government funding, but the Government Funding website, produced in response to the Treasury recommendation on a common point of access, goes some way towards this. The website has been welcomed by the sector and more details are given in **Case example 10 overleaf**.

**4.5** Other departments, whose sector funding is not currently included in the Government Funding website, have introduced initiatives of their own to improve the information available about their funding streams.

**4.6** Departments have also made various changes to the application processes for funding, aimed at helping TSOs to match their applications to the available funding, reduce the time they spend on applications and/or guide them through the process. As with the guidance that departments issue to their own funders, there is no evidence of a standardised or comprehensive approach. Departments may make use of one or more of the following:

- **internet-based information** on funding, sometimes including scope for **electronic applications** – for example, the Department for International Development's Development Awareness Fund and Civil Society Challenge Fund allow applications for funding to be submitted by e-mail, while the Department for Work and Pensions publishes electronic invitations to tender;

- **two-stage application processes**, in which a simple initial application or 'expression of interest' is used to produce a shortlist of organisations who are then asked to submit full proposals **(see Case example 11)**;

- **shorter and simpler application forms**;

- **guidance seminars** on how to apply for funding;

- clarification of **eligibility criteria** to deter speculative applications for funding, e.g. through written guidance or check-lists;

- **helplines** for funding applicants, offering advice on how to complete the application forms and whether the funding scheme is appropriate for the particular project proposed;

- giving and receiving **feedback** about the bidding process, particularly to unsuccessful applicants;

- **devolution** of responsibility for small grants to local bodies; and

- building in **grant funding for the bid-planning** process.

**4.7** A few departments were expecting to make future changes to funding information and application processes. At the Department for Environment, Food and Rural Affairs, for example, changes to sector funding were subject to the outcome of the department's wider review of rural policy, while the Department for Education and Skills' Children, Young People and Families Directorate was expecting to develop common processes across its funding programmes.

## CASE EXAMPLE 10

### Government Funding portal

Launched in September 2003 by the Active Communities Unit of the Home Office, the Government Funding website (www.governmentfunding.org.uk) provides information on grant funding available to TSOs from four government departments (the Department for Education and Skills, the Department of Health, the Office of the Deputy Prime Minister and the Home Office) and the nine Government Offices for the Regions in England, totalling £212.5 million. TSOs can search for appropriate funding schemes, download application forms and guidance notes and discuss their experiences with other TSOs. Since the site was launched, over 14,000 users have registered and TSOs feel that the site is a very useful tool. It is administered on behalf of the Home Office by the Directory of Social Change.

The Home Office is aiming for 90 per cent of grant funding distributed by the four departments and the GOs to be available via the portal. There is no data yet to assess progress against this aim.

The scope of the portal was restricted to four departments and the Government Offices after a change of contractor cut the time available to deliver the project. In future, the Home Office plans to expand the scope of the site by including details of grant funding from other departments and local government, in line with the original project plans. There will also be an increase in the number of forms which can be completed on-line. The Home Office is testing software which will allow departments to process grant applications electronically.

## CASE EXAMPLE 11

### Department of Health 'Section 64' funding – improving the application process

In April 2004 the Department of Health introduced a two-stage application process for its Section 64 General Scheme of Grants funding, which is distributed to TSO recipients direct from the Department rather than via the National Health Service. 'Section 64' funding accounts for £17.8 million health and social care funding to TSOs and aims to fund projects with national impact.

The new process requires applicants to submit only a short outline proposal using an on-line application form at the first stage. If they are successful at this stage, they are then asked to submit 'comprehensive' applications involving information that is much more detailed. All information, both the application forms and supporting documentation, is submitted through a web-based system. In parallel with the new application process, the Department has also clarified its guidance on the requirements for Section 64 funding, and informs unsuccessful applicants about the reasons for their failure.

The first set of applications under the new system was processed during 2004. The new processes have been welcomed by TSOs, who particularly praised the two-stage application process.

## TSOs' views are mixed

**4.8** The Home Office's survey of TSOs in late 2003, which covered the sector's experiences in 2002-03, found that access to information about funding was one of the more positive aspects highlighted by the sector, although a fifth of respondents were dissatisfied, and a third were dissatisfied with the information available about National Health Service funding **(Figure 16)**. This survey was carried out only around six months after departments had begun to take any action on the recommendations of the Treasury Review, so it is unlikely to have picked up the TSOs' response to new initiatives.

**4.9** The same survey found that around two-thirds of TSOs were satisfied or neutral about the process of applying for funding, with European Union funding being a particular source of dissatisfaction **(Figure 17 overleaf)**.

**4.10** TSOs we consulted during 2004 generally felt that information and application processes for government funding had not changed significantly since 2002, and in some cases had even worsened. Only a minority of respondents to the on-line consultation carried out by NCVO said processes had improved. TSOs said that:

- different government departments, or different parts of the same department, adopted **inconsistent approaches** to funding information and application requirements. The Government Funding website (see Case example 10 on page 40) was a step forward in addressing this;

- funders did not make clear **how much funding was available in total,** which would help organisations to decide where to prioritise their bids;

- **application forms** were often very lengthy and were not proportionate to the amount of funding applied for;

- the **complex language** sometimes used in application forms could deter applicants, as could electronic access only to forms;

- TSOs had to **request feedback** from funders on their applications, rather than receiving it automatically.[48]

**4.11** Those TSOs who had noticed an improvement in application processes primarily mentioned the Department of Health's changes to Section 64 funding (see Case example 11 on page 42). The Big Lottery Fund also provides an example of what can be done to streamline the application process for funds **(Case example 12 overleaf)**.

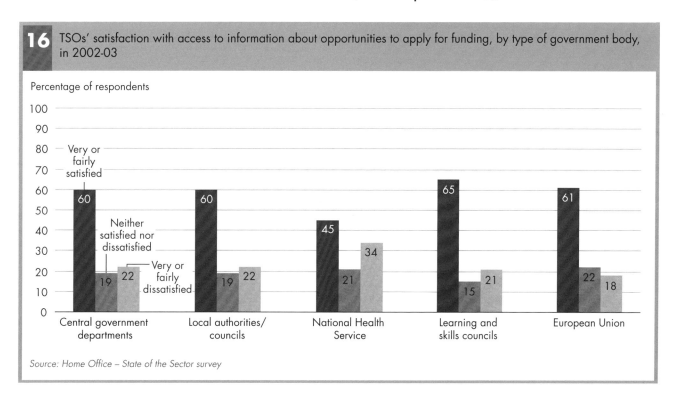

**16** TSOs' satisfaction with access to information about opportunities to apply for funding, by type of government body, in 2002-03

Percentage of respondents

Very or fairly satisfied

Neither satisfied nor dissatisfied

Very or fairly dissatisfied

| | Central government departments | Local authorities/ councils | National Health Service | Learning and skills councils | European Union |
|---|---|---|---|---|---|
| Very or fairly satisfied | 60 | 60 | 45 | 65 | 61 |
| Neither satisfied nor dissatisfied | 19 | 19 | 21 | 15 | 22 |
| Very or fairly dissatisfied | 22 | 22 | 34 | 21 | 18 |

Source: Home Office – State of the Sector survey

---

48      It should be noted, however, that in some cases where funders may receive hundreds of applications, it may not be practical to provide feedback to all applicants.

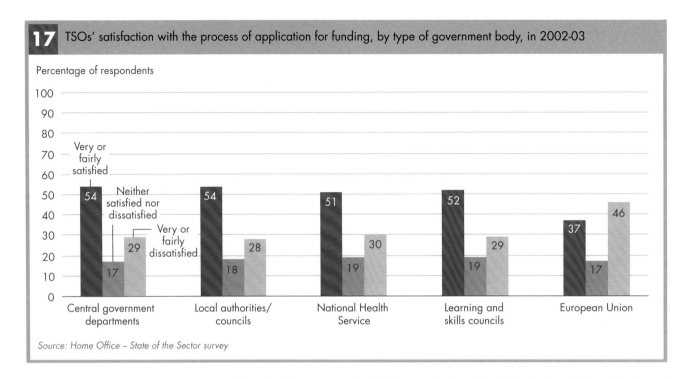

**17** TSOs' satisfaction with the process of application for funding, by type of government body, in 2002-03

Percentage of respondents

Very or fairly satisfied

Neither satisfied nor dissatisfied

Very or fairly dissatisfied

| | Central government departments | Local authorities/ councils | National Health Service | Learning and skills councils | European Union |
|---|---|---|---|---|---|
| Very or fairly satisfied | 54 | 54 | 51 | 52 | 37 |
| Neither satisfied nor dissatisfied | 17 | 18 | 19 | 19 | 17 |
| Very or fairly dissatisfied | 29 | 28 | 30 | 29 | 46 |

Source: Home Office – State of the Sector survey

## CASE EXAMPLE 12

### Big Lottery Fund application processes

Big Lottery Fund (formed in 2004 by an administrative merger between the Community Fund and the New Opportunities Fund) supports 'community transformation', from smaller grants at local level through to big capital projects, which are intended to regenerate and revitalise communities. Around 60 per cent of the £700 million distributed by Big Lottery Fund goes to TSOs through a variety of funding programmes.

Big Lottery Fund provides online information and application forms for all its funding streams, including the minimum requirements that applicants must reach in order to be considered for funding and a description of the aims of funding. Regional training seminars and a helpline are available to assist prospective applicants.

The 'Awards for All' scheme makes small grants of between £500 - £5,000 and has a simplified application form consisting of only 18 questions. The scheme aims to process all applications within eight weeks.

**4.12** The issues TSOs raised are similar to those identified in the 2003 National Audit Office report on Difficult Forms, covering forms used by individuals rather than TSOs.[49] A similar detailed evaluation of application forms for sector funding would highlight the isolated examples of best practice and help government bodies to simplify the funding application process for TSOs.

**18** Difficulties with application processes – examples from the National Audit Office research

A TSO training organisation, based in London, submitted an application for funding from a government body to provide information technology (IT) training for disadvantaged women. The application was rejected on the grounds that it was submitted in the wrong font size.

*"I was trying to lay it out nicely and I took it down to point 11, forgetting totally that at the top it had said it had to be 12 point, and it was thrown out on that. I cried."*

A small TSO based in the East Midlands, which provides education and training for women from ethnic minorities, said it had been deterred from making applications by lengthy forms:

*"There's a fund called the Community Chest[50] (part of the Single Communities Programme funded by the Neighbourhood Renewal Unit of the Office of the Deputy Prime Minister) which has hardly been touched because (of) the application process…it's very time-consuming…they're small amounts of money, £2,500 or £5,000. You think 'Do we put the effort into that application or do we put the effort into a bigger application?'".*

A national charity working with inner-city young people said that while some funders would give details of the total funding available and the likely number of applicants, others would not:

*"Some of the pots, like for instance Connexions, you don't know how much you're bidding in for…if there was only £40,000 there and you bid in for £8,000, you were (always) going to be totally unsuccessful. They were looking for the small £500 (bids)."*

Source: National Audit Office

---

49 'Difficult Forms: How government agencies interact with citizens', HC 1145, Parlimentary Session 2002-2003.
50 This comment conflicts, however, with the findings of a previous National Audit Office report on the Neighbourhood Renewal Programme, which found that the small grants available under Community Chest were widely welcomed by community groups.

## 'Passporting' information shows potential

**4.13** So-called 'passporting' – sharing information on TSOs between funders – is being trialled with the aim of reducing the burden of application processes on TSOs. The most prominent example of passporting is the pilot 'lead funder'[51] scheme launched by the Department for Work and Pensions in January 2004. Under the scheme, the Department has taken the role of lead funder, joining with Jobcentre Plus and the Learning and Skills Council to share information on two national TSOs (The Prince's Trust and Nacro (formerly the National Council for the Rehabilitation of Offenders)) and two regionally based TSOs (Project Fullemploy in London and Future Prospects in Yorkshire and Humberside).

**4.14** The passporting trial was based on a website holding a variety of information on the TSOs. The information held was of the type which TSOs are often required to submit as part of their application for funding. It ranged from basic details of the organisation, such as name and address, through full annual reports, corporate plans and policies, legal and insurance certification. All the documents can be easily downloaded from the website.

**4.15** Initial results have been positive. The website has reduced bureaucracy for the TSOs, cutting between half an hour and an hour from each funding application. The Prince's Trust and Nacro, both large organisations with networks of local offices across the UK, reported that the website had helped them to ensure that funding applications from different offices were consistent.

**4.16** However, the pilot scheme has not been able to deliver one of its hoped-for aims – that the lead funder (the Department for Work and Pensions) would validate the TSOs' documentation on behalf of other funders. The project team said this had not been achieved primarily because of funders' concerns that they would be held accountable for decisions made on the basis of information validated by other organisations. Other factors included the lack of geographical alignment between funding bodies and the lack of capacity within funding and monitoring teams to deal with other funders' complex and changing procedures.

**4.17** Meanwhile, as this report was published work was underway to establish a comprehensive national database of information about charities' activities and finances. The GuideStar UK website, funded by a £2.9 million grant from the Treasury and Cabinet Office, was expected to be launched in late summer 2005. One of its aims is to ease the passporting of information between funders.

## There has been less success in streamlining processes for assessing results

**4.18** Once funding has been awarded and the funded TSO is carrying out its work, funders will need to check that the funding is being used for the purpose that was intended. They may require the funded TSO to provide progress reports supported by documentary evidence, or visit the TSO to carry out inspections. In some cases, this monitoring of spending is combined with an assessment of the results of a project, particularly where later payments are contingent on results.

**4.19** If a TSO has several funders, each with their own monitoring system, these requirements can quickly become burdensome. The problem is exacerbated where the same monitoring requirements are applied regardless of the size of the grant or contract. TSOs we consulted felt that funders often required the same information from them, but presented in a slightly different format. The Treasury Review recognised that monitoring and evaluation requirements should be simplified and streamlined. It recommended that government should take forward the 'passporting' of financial information about third sector service providers between different departments, including developing the 'lead funder' concept (see paragraph 4.21 overleaf).

**4.20** The Treasury's subsequent guidance to funders[52] expanded on this recommendation, recommending that funding bodies should co-ordinate monitoring and inspection arrangements, by carrying out joint inspections or sharing information on recipients. The guidance also said that monitoring should be proportionate to the sums involved and the perceived risk.

---

51     www.dwp.gov.uk/leadfunder.
52     *'Guidance to Funders'*, see previous references and bibliography.

## The 'lead funder' model has not yet improved monitoring and evaluation

**4.21** The Department for Work and Pensions 'lead funder' pilot scheme described earlier in this report has been unsuccessful in its attempts to deliver joint monitoring of the results of funding. Two of the funders involved – Learning and Skills Council and Jobcentre Plus – had fundamentally different approaches to monitoring which could not be combined. While the Learning and Skills Council used a risk-based monitoring approach and visited each TSO supplier two or three times per year, Jobcentre Plus visited each supplier much more frequently, up to 22 times per year. The two organisations had different approaches to quality management and audit. Meanwhile, The Prince's Trust also said that the lead funder project had not delivered the expected improvements to monitoring and evaluation of its funding.

**4.22** Three further 'regional' lead funder pilot schemes are being held, led by Bristol City Council, Connexions and the Big Lottery Fund. The results of these projects are expected to be published by the end of 2005 and will help to show whether the lead funder model can streamline monitoring and evaluation, despite the lack of success in the national pilot scheme.

## Departments are moving towards risk-based monitoring

**4.23** We found that most departments (11 of the 13 we surveyed) had made some move towards lighter touch monitoring in recent years, for one or more of their funding streams. In most cases, changes to monitoring and evaluation processes had been initiated by funding programme teams, with the chosen approach tailored to the particular scheme. The extent of reform varied, with some departments merely trialling risk-based monitoring in one funding stream, while others had modified their project monitoring across several funding streams. There was little evidence of department-wide initiatives, although the Department for Education and Skills stressed the need for 'proportionate monitoring' through its internal guidance to funders. Apart from the lead funder pilot scheme discussed above, we found no evidence of joint working between departments to improve monitoring and evaluation.

**4.24** Changes made by departments to their monitoring processes included:

- **'risk-based' inspection,** where inspections are made on the basis of a variety of risk criteria (e.g. size of payments, opportunities for duplicate payment, size of organisation);

- **reducing the frequency** of routine inspection, but combining this with 'crisis intervention' where required, and/or reducing the frequency of project monitoring reports which TSOs are required to submit;

- **'preferred Supplier'** pilot schemes, to reduce the inspection of suppliers who demonstrate outstanding performance;

- making use of **TSOs' own monitoring and evaluation procedures,** rather than imposing extra systems;

- allowing **TSOs to decide the form and content** of reports to the funder;

- greater reliance on **personal contact** and visits than written reports.

## …but their initiatives have not yet made life easier for many TSOs

**4.25** The Home Office's survey in late 2003, carried out shortly after departments had begun to take action on the recommendations of the Treasury Review, found that around 80 per cent of TSOs it consulted were satisfied or neutral about funders' monitoring and evaluation processes, although a third were dissatisfied with these processes for European Union funding **(Figure 19)**.

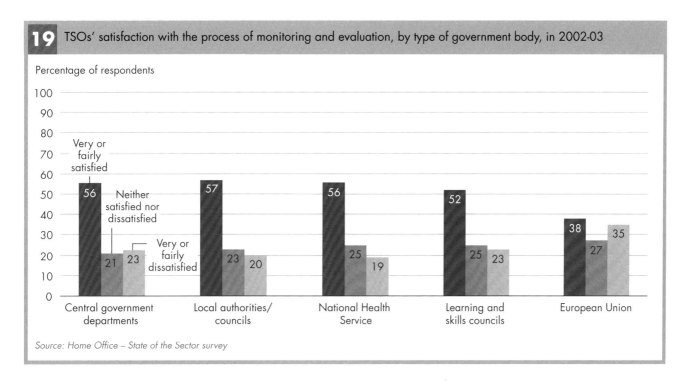

**19** TSOs' satisfaction with the process of monitoring and evaluation, by type of government body, in 2002-03

Percentage of respondents

| | Central government departments | Local authorities/ councils | National Health Service | Learning and skills councils | European Union |
|---|---|---|---|---|---|
| Very or fairly satisfied | 56 | 57 | 56 | 52 | 38 |
| Neither satisfied nor dissatisfied | 21 | 23 | 25 | 25 | 27 |
| Very or fairly dissatisfied | 23 | 20 | 19 | 23 | 35 |

Source: Home Office – State of the Sector survey

**4.26** However, in 2004, despite the evidence of departments' efforts to improve their monitoring and evaluation procedures, TSOs we consulted felt that there were still significant problems with monitoring processes. The majority of respondents (61 per cent) to our survey said monitoring processes had never been proportionate and had not improved since 2002. Their main issues were:

- lack of flexibility in target setting, including:

  - targets set at the beginning of a contract for a new service, when limited knowledge was available, but stuck to rigidly rather than being revised and reviewed on the basis of experience;

  - unrealistic targets;

  - lack of scope for qualitative measures of output;

- lack of proportionality in monitoring (such that a £5,000 grant would be monitored in the same way as a £50,000 grant);

- variation even within the same initiative on the level of information that is sought;

- over-performance, whereby restrictions could be placed on future funding due to meeting targets.

**4.27** However, there are some examples of funders taking steps to introduce lighter-touch monitoring and evaluation schemes, which have been welcomed by the sector (**Case example 13**).

## CASE EXAMPLE 13

**The Heritage Lottery Fund**

The Heritage Lottery Fund aims to make heritage activity accessible and enjoyable for all sections of society. In 2003-04 approximately £300,000 was paid out to TSOs through three categories of grant. When awarding grants, risk assessment is made according to factors such as the experience and size of the TSO and the nature of the project. All recipients of funding must send back proof of expenditure and an annual project monitoring report, which asks questions on the progress made and plans for dealing with any cost escalation. Heritage Lottery Fund appoint monitors for larger and higher risk grants, who liaise with the TSO through site visits and produce their own reports for the Heritage Lottery Fund.

## There is scope for better audit and inspection

**4.28** TSOs' funding relationships with government funders are subject not only to monitoring and evaluation by funders of the results of the project, but also to audit as part of processes to ensure that public money is correctly spent. These audits are carried out principally by the TSO's auditors or the funders' own internal audit departments, and sometimes by other bodies such as the National Audit Office (in the case of central government spending) and the Audit Commission (responsible for the audit of local government spending). The cost of audit certificates – formal proof, provided by a TSO's financial auditor, that grant monies have been spent on the purposes for which they were provided – could be a significant drain on TSOs' resources if multiple funders each require an audit certificate. Audit certificates typically cost around £1,000 for a small TSO.

**4.29** Clarification is still needed on the reasons for the apparently widespread reluctance by funders to collaborate on audit and inspection of funding recipients; for example, by sharing audit certificates. A pilot project is underway in the West Midlands region, involving the National Audit Office, the Audit Commission and local funders (the Government Office for the West Midlands, Advantage West Midlands, the Learning and Skills Council, Connexions, Birmingham City Council, Big Lottery Fund and the Legal Services Commission) to examine the scope for joint audit processes. The pilot aims to reduce duplication and unnecessary bureaucratic burdens by streamlining monitoring, evaluation and audit processes. The project, known as the Combined Audit National Pilot, has developed an agreed audit process which will be tested with a number of funders and recipients during 2005.

# APPENDIX 1

## Treasury 2002 Review recommendations

Note: the 2002 Review used the terms "voluntary and community sector (VCS)" and "voluntary and community organisation (VCO)", while this report refers to "the third sector" and "third sector organisation (TSO)".

| Recommendation | Responsibility and timing | Outcome |
|---|---|---|
| Issue: Weaknesses in the data on government funding of the VCS. | | |
| **12** Government should establish a unified information system for data collection and analysis on government funding for the VCS. | The Active Communities Unit (ACU) of the Home Office will lead cross-departmental work to put in place a unified information system. This will involve: (i) scoping and piloting; (ii) phased introduction according to defined milestones; and (iii) the development of individual strands to support implementation of the review, including data on the Compact, on capacity building and infrastructure, and on funding going to the sector. By: **April 2006** | ACU collates data on government funding of the VCS, via departments' standardised returns to Charities' Aid Foundation, ACU's contractor. Unified information system not yet in place. |
| Issue: Full cost recovery. | | |
| **13** Funders should recognise that it is legitimate for providers to include the relevant element of overheads in their cost estimates for providing a given service under service agreement or contract. | All departments will incorporate the review's funding recommendations fully into their procurement policies by ensuring that the price for contracts reflects the full cost of the service, including the legitimate portion of overhead costs. By: **April 2006** | Not achieved at the time of writing this report (see main text). |
| **14** Central government should learn from the experience of programmes that have already sought to tackle this issue in a fair and transparent way. | DfES, working with OGC and ACU, building on experience to date and on work being undertaken by DfES as part of 'Getting the Best from Each Other', will develop guidance for good practice in the procurement of services. This work will contribute to a supplement to the Compact Code of Good Practice on Funding for service contracts and agreements. All departments and agencies will agree a common approach in line with this guidance and Treasury guidance in preparation for implementation from April 2004. By: **October 2003** | 'Compact Code of Good Practice on Funding and Procurement' published in March 2005. |
| | The Department for Culture, Media and Sport will consider amending the rules and working practices of the lottery distributors in order to reflect the key recommendations of the review. By: **April 2003** | The Department is encouraging lottery distributors to adopt the recommendations of the review. In February 2005, the Big Lottery Fund (formed by a merger between the New Opportunities Fund and the Community Fund in 2004) announced that it would adopt the principle of full cost recovery in all its grant-making. |

| Recommendation | Responsibility and timing | Outcome |
|---|---|---|
| **15** The VCS should develop accounting guidelines for allocating overhead costs.<br><br>**16** The VCS should consider building on the experience of larger voluntary organisations to establish whether there is a useful role for benchmarking unit costs in client specific service areas. | The VCS will produce guidance for the sector, building on the work currently being undertaken by ACEVO, and to consider (in consultation with the Charity Commission), the scope for linking to SORP guidance. By: **April 2003** | Produced by ACEVO as 'Funding our Future II: Understand and Allocate Costs', 2002. Revised and updated as 'Full Cost Recovery: a guide and toolkit on cost allocation', ACEVO and New Philanthropy Capital 2004. |

Issue: Streamlining access and performance management requirements for multiple, often small, funding streams.

| | | |
|---|---|---|
| **17** Government should develop a common point of access and a common application process for central government grant aid and strategic funding. | The ACU will build on its Invest to Save project to develop an electronic portal to give a common point of access to Government grant funding for the VCS in order to provide a common application process. By: **April 2004** | www.governmentfunding.org.uk website – see description earlier in this report. |
| **18** Government should take forward the "passporting" of financial information about VCS service providers between different departments, including developing the "lead funder" concept. | Over the medium term, the portal may also be used to passport information about VCOs. "Passporting" is the transfer of basic details of organisations between funders, reducing the burden of providing the same information more than once. By: **April 2004**<br><br>On 'lead funder', the Regional Coordination Unit of the Office of the Deputy Prime Minister (RCU), working with DfES and the ACU, will develop examples of how the 'lead funder' approach could be applied in practice across government departments. The RCU, ACU and NRU will consider piloting the approach with regeneration funds and with the DWP from **April 2004**. | Lead Funder Pilot details given earlier in this report. |

Issue: End loading of payments – with sector bearing all the upfront cost and risk.

| | | |
|---|---|---|
| **19** The Treasury should issue clear guidance to funders: (i) on the scope for making payments in advance of expenditure; (ii) ensuring the right balance of risk between service providers and funders; and (iii) the potential use of profile funding. | The Treasury will publish guidance to funders. By: **December 2002** | 'Guidance to Funders' issued 2003. |
| **20** Umbrella groups within VCS should raise awareness within the sector and government of the principles set out in the guidance. | The dissemination programme will begin from April 2003. By: **April 2006** | VCS groups have raised funders' awareness of the guidance. |

| Recommendation | Responsibility and timing | Outcome |
|---|---|---|
| Issue: Achieving a more stable funding relationship. | | |
| **21** The Treasury guidance to funders should underline the opportunities for moving to more stable funding relationships and to include examples of where, subject to performance, this has been done. | The Treasury will include in its guidance to funders. By: **December 2002** | See above. |
| Issue: Implementation of the Compact. | | |
| **27** All government departments should appoint a senior official to oversee full implementation of the Compact and Codes. | Senior officials will be appointed by all departments. By: **October 2002** | Achieved at the time of writing this report. |
| **28** The ACU should conduct a review of the role of the Voluntary Sector Liaison Officer and determine the scope of the role to support and maintain mainstreaming of the Compact and Codes. | The review will be completed and the findings will feed in to departmental strategies for mainstreaming of the Compact and Codes. By: **January 2003** | Achieved at the time of writing this report. |
| **29** The 'Champion' should establish a baseline on awareness and implementation in their department and develop a strategy for mainstreaming the Compact. | Departmental "Champions" will produce a strategy and project plan for delivering the strategy. By: **April 2003**<br><br>Given the major role of the Government Offices in allocating central resources, the ACU working with the RCU will ensure that staff in the regional offices are made fully aware of the implications of the Compact for their dealings with the sector. Starting in **April 2003** | Departmental strategies were delivered to ACU during 2004 and early 2005. Government Offices aware of the implications of the Compact. |

# APPENDIX 2
## Glossary

| | |
|---|---|
| **ACEVO** | Association of Chief Executives of Voluntary Organisations. |
| **Active Communities Directorate (ACD)** | The Home Office directorate responsible for the achievement of the Government's target of increasing VCS involvement in public services by 5 per cent by 2006. The ACD leads work across government to implement the recommendations of the 2002 Treasury Review, and most recently has been responsible for the launch of the Compact Plus proposals in March 2005. |
| **Active Communities Unit (ACU)** | One of three units (with the Volunteering and Charitable Giving Unit, and the Charities Unit) which together make up the Active Communities Directorate of the Home Office. |
| **BGOP** | Better Government for Older People, an initiative funded by DWP. |
| **BRTF** | Better Regulation Task Force. An independent body that advises Government on action to ensure that regulation and its enforcement accord with the five Principles of Good Regulation. |
| **CO** | Cabinet Office. |
| **(The) Compact** | An understanding between government and the third sector on how they should work together, agreed in 1998. |
| **CRCSG** | Crime Reduction and Community Safety Group, part of the Home Office. |
| **Cross-Cutting Review/ Treasury Review** | 'The Role of the Voluntary and Community Sector in Service Delivery: A Cross-Cutting Review'. Part of the Treasury's 2002 Spending Review which explored how central and local government could work more effectively with the VCS to deliver high quality services. |
| **DCMS** | Department for Culture, Media and Sport. |
| **Deakin Commission Report** | A 1996 independent report, 'Meeting the Challenge of Change: Voluntary Action into the 21st Century', published by the National Council for Voluntary Organisations, which set out an agenda for the future development of the voluntary sector. |
| **Dear Accounting Officer (DAO) letters** | A Treasury letter to government departments' Accounting Officers which provides specific advice on issues of accountability, regularity, propriety and annual accounting exercises. They supplement the guidance published in the Government Accounting Manual and are issued by the Treasury Officer of Accounts team in the Treasury. |
| **Defra** | Department for Environment, Food and Rural Affairs. |

| | |
|---|---|
| **DETR/DTLR** | Department of Environment, Transport and the Regions/Department for Transport, Local Government and the Regions. In June 2001, DETR's environment portfolio became the responsibility of the newly formed Defra. Responsibility for local government, the regions and transport was passed to DTLR. In May 2002, DTLR's transport functions became the responsibility of the new Department for Transport and most non-transport functions passed to the new ODPM. |
| **DfEE/DfES** | Department for Education and Employment/Department for Education and Skills. |
| **DfID** | Department for International Development. |
| **DoH** | Department of Health. |
| **DSS/DWP** | Department of Social Security/Department for Work and Pensions. |
| **DTI** | Department of Trade and Industry. |
| **DTLR** | Department for Transport, Local Government and the Regions (see DETR/DTLR above). |
| **ESF** | European Social Fund. |
| **FCO** | Foreign and Commonwealth Office. |
| **Full cost recovery** | Costing activities to include the appropriate share of overhead or indirect costs, as well as the direct costs of delivering a service. |
| **Futurebuilders** | A government investment fund, launched in 2004, which uses loan finance to increase the role that the third sector plays in public service delivery. |
| **GO** | Government Office for the Regions. There are nine GOs in England. |
| **Grade 3 Champion** | The senior civil servant responsible for strategic direction and high level implementation of the Treasury Review's recommendations relevant to his or her department. |
| **HO** | Home Office. |
| **IR** | Inland Revenue, now HM Revenue and Customs. |
| **LCD/DCA** | Lord Chancellor's Department/Department for Constitutional Affairs. |
| **LDA** | London Development Agency. |
| **LSC** | Learning and Skills Council. |
| **MAFF/Defra** | Ministry of Agriculture, Fisheries and Food/Department for Environment, Food and Rural Affairs. |
| **Match funding** | A requirement by funding agencies that any contributions they make towards programme or project costs should be matched by other funders, or by the applicants from their own resources. Some funders allow in-kind contributions (e.g. the value of volunteer time) to count. |
| **MoD** | Ministry of Defence. |
| **NACVS** | National Association of Councils for Voluntary Service. |

| | |
|---|---|
| NAO | National Audit Office. |
| NCVO | National Council for Voluntary Organisations. |
| ODPM | Office of the Deputy Prime Minister. |
| Nacro | National Association for the Care and Rehabilitation of Offenders. |
| NDPB | Non-Departmental Public Body. |
| NRU | Neighbourhood Renewal Unit, part of ODPM. |
| OGC | Office of Government Commerce. The government's advisor on procurement and project management. |
| PPAs | Partnership Programme Agreements, a series of long-term funding agreements between DfID and major TSOs involved in international development. |
| PSA target | Public Service Agreement target, set by central government for key service improvements across government. |
| RCU | Regional Co-ordination Unit, part of ODPM. |
| RNID | Royal National Institute for the Deaf. |
| Section 64 funding | The main funding stream for Department of Health grants, referring to the grant-making powers given to the Secretary of State for Health under Section 64 of the Health Services and Public Health Act 1968. |
| Charity SORP | Charity Statement of Recommended Practice. The accounting standard to which registered charities in England and Wales should conform. |
| Spending Review | A statement of the government's spending plans for a particular period. |
| Treasury Review | See Cross-Cutting Review above. |
| TSO | Third Sector Organisation. This term refers both to small not-for-profit organisations working on a local level and dependent on voluntary effort as well as larger not-for-profit organisations working on a regional, national and international level with paid staff. Both registered charities and other not-for-profit organisations are included in the third sector. |
| VCSLO | Voluntary and Community Sector Liaison Officer. The mid-ranking civil servant responsible for monitoring the implementation of the Treasury Review recommendations relevant to his or her department and working with the Grade 3 Champion. |

# APPENDIX 3
## Methodology

The study examined three issues:

- What progress have the individual departments made against the recommendations of the Treasury Review?

- What is the sector's perspective on progress to date?

- What are the key challenges and potential solutions?

The NAO team's research focused primarily on departments' progress, while our partner, NCVO, researched the sector's perspective. Key challenges and potential solutions were developed from the results of both streams of work.

## NAO research

### Consultation with stakeholders and key interest groups

We consulted widely during the planning and fieldwork stages of our study, seeking views on the three issues above. Throughout the study we liaised closely with the Active Communities Directorate of the Home Office, and the Home Office-led groups responsible for leading and monitoring central government's implementation of the VCS funding commitment (including the Programme Implementation Group, Grade 3 Champions Group, VCSLO Network and the Home Office Voluntary and Community Sector Advisory Group). We also worked with the Treasury.

Other groups and individuals we consulted included:

- Association of Chief Executives of Voluntary Organisations (ACEVO)

- Audit Commission

- Better Regulation Task Force

- The Charity Commission

- Charity Finance Directors' Group

- The Dyslexia Institute

- Futurebuilders

- IDeA (the Innovation and Development Agency for local government)

- International Society for Third Sector Research

- Joseph Rowntree Foundation

- Julia Unwin, independent consultant

- Leonard Cheshire

- Local Government Association

- National Association of Councils for Voluntary Service (NACVS)

- National Lead Funder Pilot

- New Philanthropy Capital

- Office of Public Management

- Tom Kennar, independent government consultant

- Turning Point

## Survey of government departments

We carried out a survey of 13 central government departments, focusing on those departments with the largest funding responsibilities for the third sector, but also including some smaller funders where involvement with the third sector was relatively new (for example, the Inland Revenue, now HM Revenue and Customs). The survey focused on progress on the key issues covered by the Treasury Review. Where appropriate, we also issued the survey to departments' NDPBs and executive agencies, and to the Government Offices for the Regions. We followed up the survey responses with discussions with the departments' Voluntary and Community Sector Liaison Officers, finance staff and funding programme managers. We also reviewed departments' third sector strategies, funding policies and other documents relating to their funding of the third sector.

## Focus groups

We commissioned MORI to undertake a series of four focus groups with programme managers and finance staff in government funding bodies, on the degree to which the Treasury Review's recommendations had been adopted, and any barriers they faced in changing their day-to-day funding practices.

## Expert workshops

We held two workshops involving a range of leading experts on government funding and TSO finance, focusing on full cost recovery and the 'grant or contract?' decision.

## NCVO research

We commissioned NCVO to undertake a range of qualitative and quantitative research with the third sector, including:

- a web-based consultation which attracted more than 140 detailed responses, to establish the key themes in TSO experience of funding relationships with the government;

- more in-depth research to build on the consultation:

    - nine face-to-face interviews with the chief executives of a range of TSOs;

    - seven focus groups, held in locations around England, to discuss progress with the Treasury Review recommendations from the VCS perspective;

- two open consultation workshops, in Birmingham and London, to explore the research findings further;

- a review of the relevant literature, including international comparisons to compare experiences with other developed countries where VCOs are funded to deliver public services.

# APPENDIX 4
## Bibliography

We drew on a range of relevant publications in researching this report, including the following key sources:

## Government reports and guidance on third sector funding

*The Compact on relations between the government and the voluntary and community sector,* Home Office, 1998

*Funding and Procurement: Compact Code of Good Practice,* Home Office, 2005

*The role of the voluntary and community sector in service delivery: a cross cutting review,* HM Treasury, 2002

*Guidance to funders: improving funding relationships for voluntary and community organisations,* HM Treasury, 2003

*Think Smart...Think Voluntary Sector! Good practice guidance on procurement of services from the voluntary and community sector,* Home Office, 2004

*Exploring the role of the third sector in public service delivery and reform: a discussion document,* HM Treasury, 2005

*Central Government Funding of Voluntary and Community Organisations 1982-83 to 2001-02,* Home Office, 2004

## Other stakeholders

*Meeting the Challenge of Change: Voluntary Action into the 21st Century,* National Council for Voluntary Organisations, 1996

*Funding Our Future II: Understand and Allocate Costs,* Association of Chief Executives of Voluntary Organisations and New Philanthropy Capital, 2002

*Surer Funding, ACEVO Commission of Inquiry Report,* Association of Chief Executives of Voluntary Organisations, 2004

*The Grant-making Tango: Issues for Funders,* Baring Foundation, 2004

*Shared aspirations: the role of the voluntary and community sector in improving the funding relationship with government,* National Council for Voluntary Organisations, 2005

*The UK Voluntary Sector Almanac 2004,* National Council for Voluntary Organisations, 2004

## Other reports

*Releasing Resources for the Frontline: Independent Review of Public Sector Efficiency,* HM Treasury, 2004

# REPORTS BY THE COMPTROLLER AND AUDITOR GENERAL, SESSION 2005-2006

*The Comptroller and Auditor General has to date, in Session 2005-2006, presented to the House of Commons the following reports under Section 9 of the National Audit Act, 1983. The reports are listed by subject category.*

|  |  | **Publication date** |
|---|---|---|
| **Cross-Government** |  |  |
| Home Office: Working with the Third Sector | HC 75 | 29 June 2005 |
| **Defence** |  |  |
| Driving the Successful Delivery of Major Defence Projects: Effective Project Control is a Key Factor in Successful Projects | HC 30 | 20 May 2005 |
| Managing the Defence Estate | HC 25 | 25 May 2005 |
| Assessing and Reporting Military Readiness | HC 72 | 15 June 2005 |
| **Education** |  |  |
| Securing strategic leadership for the learning and skills sector in England | HC 29 | 18 May 2005 |
| **Environment, Food and Rural Affairs** |  |  |
| Lost in Translation? Responding to the challenges of European law | HC 26 | 26 May 2005 |
| Environment Agency: Efficiency in water resource management | HC 73 | 17 June 2005 |
| **Law, Order and Central** |  |  |
| Public Guardianship Office: Protecting and promoting the financial affairs of people who lose mental capacity | HC 27 | 8 June 2005 |
| **National Health Service** |  |  |
| Innovation in the NHS: Local Improvement Finance Trusts | HC 28 | 19 May 2005 |
| The Refinancing of the Norfolk and Norwich PFI Hospital: how the deal can be viewed in the light of the refinancing | HC 78 | 10 June 2005 |
| **Revenue departments** |  |  |
| Filing of Income Tax Self Assessment Returns | HC 74 | 22 June 2005 |

Printed in the UK for the Stationery Office Limited
on behalf of the Controller of Her Majesty's Stationery Office
179929   06/05   77240